D0282485

FORGING

A

UNION

OF

STEEL

Philip Murray, SWOC, and the
United Steelworkers

Paul F. Clark, Peter Gottlieb, and Donald Kennedy
Editors

ILR Press
New York State School of
Industrial and Labor Relations
Cornell University

© 1987 by Cornell University
All rights reserved
Cover design: Kat Dalton

Library of Congress Cataloging in Publication Data will be found at the end of this book.

Material in "Battling over Government's Role" that appeared in Ronald Schatz, "Philip Murray and the Subordination of the Industrial Union to the United States Government," *Labor Leaders in America,* is used with permission of the University of Illinois Press.

The comments by John Hoerr are adapted from his forthcoming book, *And the Wolf Finally Came: The Decline of the American Steel Industry.* They are printed with permission of the University of Pittsburgh Press.

Copies may be ordered from
ILR Press
New York State School of
Industrial and Labor Relations
Cornell University
Ithaca, New York 14851-0952

Printed in the United States of America
5 4 3 2 1

CONTENTS

PREFACE

NINETEEN eighty-six was both the fiftieth anniversary of the United Steelworkers of America and the one-hundredth anniversary of the birth of Philip Murray. In the view of many labor historians, Philip Murray, the Steel Workers' Organizing Committee (SWOC), and the United Steelworkers of America (USWA) have not received the attention their contribution to the modern American labor movement merits. The gap in the historical record regarding Murray and the organization he helped shape into the United Steelworkers of America presents a challenge and an opportunity to those interested in documenting the growth and development of American unionism in the twentieth century.

In an effort to address this issue, the Department of Labor Studies and the Historical Collections and Labor Archives at Pennsylvania State University, the United Steelworkers of America, and the Pennsylvania Humanities Council jointly sponsored a symposium on Philip Murray, SWOC, and the United Steelworkers on November 13–14, 1986. The symposium was designed to bring scholars together with individuals who had been involved in the early years of the USWA, either as active participants in the union or as informed observers of this era.

To this end, four scholarly papers were commissioned to serve as the centerpiece of the program. It was hoped that the papers would identify and begin to investigate specific issues and themes that could be pursued by historians and others interested in the contribution to American labor history of Philip Murray and the union he helped found. The historians invited to prepare these papers—David Brody of the University of California at Davis,

Melvyn Dubofsky of the State University of New York at Binghamton, Mark McColloch of the University of Pittsburgh, and
Ronald Schatz of Wesleyan University—were chosen based on
their background and interest in the topic. Their papers serve
as the basis for this publication.

Among the union participants invited to contribute to the
symposium were I. W. Abel, president of the USWA from 1965
to 1977, and Walter Burke, who served as secretary-treasurer
of the USWA during the same period. Both Abel and Burke
joined the Steelworkers in 1936 and were active as local and
district officials during the early years of SWOC and the USWA.
Invited as outside observers of the union were Abe Raskin, long-
time labor correspondent for the *New York Times,* and John Hoerr,
senior labor writer for *Business Week* magazine. Both Raskin and
Hoerr covered the USWA as journalists during much of the
period examined by the symposium. Their comments and observations, presented to the symposium as reactions to the formal
papers, are included in the publication. Also included are comments by Harold J. Ruttenberg, who from 1936 to 1946 was an
organizer and research director for SWOC and the USWA.

The introduction to this collection was written expressly for
the publication and provides background on the work, or lack
thereof, that has been done on Philip Murray and the founding
of the USWA. This section was written by Ronald Filippelli of
Pennsylvania State University.

The original purpose of this project was to focus attention on
an individual and an organization that played very significant
roles in the evolution of the modern American labor movement
and to suggest an agenda for future research in this area. The
symposium held in November 1986 was a large step in this direction. The purpose of this publication is to share the results
of that experience.

The editors would like to thank those individuals, mentioned
above, whose participation in this project is reflected in the papers
and comments that follow. We would also like to thank Richard
Trumka, president of the United Mine Workers; Lynn Williams,
president of the United Steelworkers of America; Helmut Golatz
and Alice Hoffman, both formerly with Pennsylvania State University; Nelson Lichtenstein of Catholic University; and Steven

Fraser of Basic Books for their contributions as commentators, moderators, or speakers. Finally, we are especially indebted to Russell Gibbons, then communications director of the United Steelworkers of America, for his unflagging support and consistent cooperation, both of which were critical in seeing this project through to completion.

Funding for the project was provided by the Pennsylvania Humanities Council, the United Steelworkers of America, and Pennsylvania State University.

Paul F. Clark
Department of Labor Studies
Pennsylvania State University

Peter Gottlieb
Historical Collections and Labor Archives
Pennsylvania State University

Donald Kennedy
Education Center
International Association of Machinists

THE HISTORY IS MISSING, ALMOST: PHILIP MURRAY, THE STEELWORKERS, AND THE HISTORIANS

Ronald L. Filippelli

MUCH has changed in collective bargaining in the steel industry in the past twenty years, and the United Steelworkers of
America, once one of America's premier economic, social, and
political institutions, has had to battle for its very existence. Indeed, the past twenty years of labor history in the United States,
particularly as they relate to the fortunes of the original unions
of the Congress of Industrial Organizations (CIO), make it increasingly important to encourage historians to study the history
of the Steelworkers. For if steel was the bastion of the open shop,
and its fall to the force of the Steel Workers' Organizing Committee (SWOC), more than any other labor victory of the 1930s,
symbolized the rise of organized labor to a position of power in
the United States, then might the recent sad history of labor
relations in steel also signal the end of the period of mass industrial relations ushered in by the CIO?

Walter Galenson, in his standard history of the early CIO, *The
CIO Challenge to the AFL* (1960), wrote, some twenty years after
the foundation of SWOC, that if there was any single series of
events in the labor history of the 1930s that could be characterized as having momentous import, it was the organization of the
steel industry. Paradoxically, instead of being the first of many
scholarly investigations of unionization in steel, Galenson's chapter proved to be one of the last major investigations of the subject.

That is not to say that there has been no scholarly interest in steel. A few good works have appeared on specialized topics such as the culture of the immigrant working-class community. One thinks of John Bodnar's work on the culture of immigrant steelworkers (1977) and of Charles Walker's classic (1950) on Elwood City, Pennsylvania, which are outstanding studies of working-class culture, ethnicity, and community. There have been several fine contributions on the condition of black steelworkers, notably Peter Gottlieb's (1987) and Dennis Dickerson's (1986). Several articles deal with the Little Steel strike, and there is Staughton Lynd's provocative article (1983) on the rank-and-file movement. Lloyd Ulman's study of the government of the union (1962) stands alone as an investigation of the institutional roots of the Steelworkers' centralized structure. Finally, although he is not a historian, labor journalist Jack Herling wrote a spirited account of the contested election in 1965 between I. W. Abel and David J. McDonald. Herling's *Right to Challenge* (1972) stands as labor studies' equivalent to Theodore White's *Making of the President* series.

Useful as these studies are, they hardly represent a scholarly production worthy of the importance of the subject. The paucity of scholarship is striking. There is, for example, no equivalent in steel to Peter Friedlander's provocative monograph *The Emergence of a UAW Local, 1936–1939: A Study in Class and Culture* (1975). In fact, I know of no scholarly studies of the union at the local level. Even more puzzling is the lack of a biography of Philip Murray, let alone a serious scholarly study. The bibliographical note that follows Murray's entry in Gary Fink's *Biographical Dictionary of American Labor Leaders* (1974) lists only general works on the period and a few biographical sketches in compendiums on American labor leaders. Murray is, arguably, the least known of America's great labor figures. Incredibly, a man who was at John L. Lewis's side for twenty-four years of Byzantine politics in the United Mine Workers, who led SWOC in its battles with Big Steel, and who later directed the CIO through World War II and the crucial early years of the Cold War emerges in histories of the period as nothing more than, as Irving Bernstein describes him in *The Turbulent Years* (1970, 443), "the good man of the labor movement." It is not to detract from his humanity to suggest that there must have been a good deal more to Murray then the humble, kindly, devout, one-dimensional figure of Saint Phil generally pictured. Fortunately, Ronald Schatz's chapter on Murray in Melvyn Dubofsky and Warren Van Tine's book, *The Labor Leader in America* (1987), is a start in changing this perception and reversing the neglect.

Compare this neglect with the treatment of other labor leaders of Murray's stature. There are two biographies of George Meany, dead less than a decade, though neither is scholarly. There are six of Walter Reuther at last count, four of Sidney Hillman, two of David Dubinsky, and at least half a dozen of Lewis. The lack of biographical treatment extends to Murray's lieutenants. Only Clinton Golden, SWOC's eastern director, has found his biographer in Thomas Brooks (1978).

What treatment there is of the Steelworkers in the history of the industrial union movement falls generally into two historiographical categories, delineated by David Brody in his essays on the period (1980). They can be summarized as follows: (1) The CIO was a distinct shift in the direction of American labor away from pure and simple economic unionism toward a major institutional role in the social economic, and political life of the nation at the macro level, that is, a mass movement of the American working class toward social democracy. (2) The CIO was a shift in direction away from the model of the American Federation of Labor (AFL), but to the right rather than to the left, toward a position as a junior partner of American monopoly capitalism in the reshaping of the postwar world. In this scenario, the natural militant tendencies of the rank and file were blunted and turned back, not only by a fearful management and government but also by labor leaders whose right to sit in the councils of power depended on their ability to guarantee stable, nonradical industrial relations. Brody adds a third category, which is relatively new and offers intriguing possibilities—that the CIO was essentially an extension of the AFL's pure and simple economic unionism in industrial rather than craft form—old wine in a new bottle.

Liberal Historians' View

The majority of the existing research falls into the first category. For proponents of this view—liberal historians such as Irving

Bernstein, Walter Galenson, and Robert R. Brooks, best labeled institutionalists because of their concentration on the role of institutions and their leaders—the story lay largely in the interplay between the AFL and the CIO in the debate over craft versus industrial unionism. The heroes in their accounts are not the workers, who are almost absent, but the leaders, especially Lewis, but also Murray, the Reuther brothers, Hillman, and Dubinsky, who seized the opportunity provided by the National Industrial Recovery Act (NIRA) and the Wagner Act from the faltering hands of William Green and the shortsighted AFL leaders and put the necessary money and talent into the fight.

Success, for these scholars, was achieved when there was institutional stability in the CIO, no mean feat considering the past history of organized labor in the United States. In *The Turbulent Years* (1970), Bernstein's story of the SWOC drive is one of skillful strategy and tactics, a sophisticated campaign in which the leadership maneuvered with the employee representation plans (ERPs), the company unions; the National Labor Relations Board; the Roosevelt administration; the National War Labor Board; and, with Lewis in the lead, with U.S. Steel's Myron Taylor. As Galenson pointed out (1960), what was different in this organizing drive from the failures of 1892, 1901, and 1919 was that it was funded with millions, rather than hundreds, of dollars. *Barron's* magazine (March 8, 1937) agreed that "for the first time in the history of the United States, industrial management is faced with a labor movement which is smart and courageous, wealthy and successful—a movement, moreover, which is winning its battle by applying a shrewd imitation of big business organization and technique" (page 3).

Granted the skill of the strategists, but what about the workers? At worst they appear as passive onlookers, at best as reluctant brides. Bernstein, for example, does not even bother to mention the rank-and-file movement in steel when he describes the upsurge of organizational activity following passage of the NIRA in 1933. According to Frederick Harbison, in his chapter on steel in Harry Millis's *How Collective Bargaining Works* (1942), the steelworkers had neither the leadership nor the rank-and-file enthusiasm to organize spontaneously. Indeed, SWOC was so top down that when the Little Steel strike came in 1937, the organization was ill prepared for the struggle. If one assumes that SWOC lacked indigenous leadership and militancy, it makes sense that other unions, especially the United Mine Workers, would supply it. Robert R. Brooks, in *As Steel Goes* (1940), supported Harbison's observations, noting that in few unions was the proportion of nonelected "outsiders" among the leaders so high. From Murray on down, all SWOC officers were appointed. According to Bernstein, Murray recognized that the steelworkers could contribute little to the staff at the outset because of their inexperience and fear.

A careful reading of the liberal historians indicates that the lack of enthusiasm of SWOC's leaders for the abilities of the rank and file was returned in kind. As late as 1940, according to Galenson, Murray admitted that although SWOC claimed a membership of 500,000, only half paid dues regularly. Brooks confirms this figure and says that the pattern held from 1937 to 1940. In his autobiography (1969), David McDonald indicated that the steelworkers did not rush to sign SWOC cards. What the organizers hoped would be a torrent turned out to be a trickle. McDonald attributed this low turnout to fear, the open-shop tradition, and the fact that "some workers were as apprehensive about dictatorship from an international union as they were of arm twisting from the employer" (page 93). According to Brooks, SWOC organizers blamed this fear on the continuation of anti-union policies by employers, even those who had signed SWOC contracts. Galenson, in his comparison of SWOC and the United Automobile Workers (UAW), suggested that the UAW was self-supporting because it had an active internal democracy at a time when SWOC was still a nonrepresentative organization.

The nature of the rank and file among the steelworkers is critical to the historical debate. If, as the liberal historians would have us believe, the CIO was a mass working-class movement attempting to wrest a share of power in American society, then their own accounts indicate that the workers, at least in steel, were in no hurry to enlist in the crusade.

New Left View

The nature of the rank and file was even more central to the argument of the new left and neo-Marxist historians who rose up to challenge the standard interpretation. Their conception of the labor history of the period, best characterized in the case of steel by Staughton Lynd's article in *Radical America* (1972) on the rank-and-file movement (see also Lynd 1983) and the short oral histories of organizers in steel in his and Alice Lynd's book, *Rank and File* (1973), was that the workers were self-mobilized for collective action. Rather than celebrate the triumph of the CIO, new left writers have emphasized how monopoly capital, with the complicity of the bulk of the leadership of the CIO and the government, and motivated by the failure of the Communist party, turned the spontaneous militancy of the rank and file back, institutionalized labor relations on its terms, and regained mastery of the situation. Grass-roots involvement was replaced by top-down bureaucracy. In their model, the subsequent structure and function of the union were dependent on the hegemony of capitalist social institutions. Unions thus became one of the institutions of social control, particularly at the workplace.

For Lynd and the other new left historians, the rank and file is the true subject for study, and, as David Brody wrote in commenting on Lynd's work (1985, 458), "The logic of that history resides not—as Bernstein and the liberal institutionalists would have it—in how militancy progressed to stable collective bargaining, but rather in how that process killed the rank-and-file character of industrial-union organization." For Lynd, the spontaneous appearance of union locals in the steel towns after the passage of the NIRA was the result of the efforts of rank-and-file steelworkers, with little help from full-time organizers of the feeble Amalgamated Association of Iron and Steel Workers. Far from being unsuccessful, as Galenson characterized this drive, the Rank-and-File Movement signed up about the same number of steelworkers between June 1933 and April 1934 as SWOC did, using two hundred full-time organizers, in a comparable period from June 1936 to March 1937. Why did this drive not achieve the union recognition accomplished by SWOC? According to Lynd, the steel companies, in league with the government and labor leaders, undercut the drive because of its militancy.

Nor do the Communists escape blame in the new left approach. For Lynd, the failure of the Communists to offer their leadership and support to the Rank-and-File Movement was the critical weakness of the drive. Had the Communist party moved, he wrote in 1983 (203–4), "there might have come about an industrial unionism not only more militant and more internally democratic, but also more independent politically." Indeed, William Z. Foster, leader of the 1919 steel strike and by the 1930s the general secretary of the American Communist party, wrote in *Organizing Steel,* in 1936, that the critical difference between 1919 and 1936 was the existence of a strong Communist party to assist the industrial union movement.

Why then did the Communist party not play a larger role in supporting the Rank-and-File Movement? Because, according to the new left historians, the party, in 1933 and 1934, was in its dual unionist phase in accord with the Communist International (COMINTERN) line, and rote obedience to the line meant that they would not work within the Amalgamated, regardless of the cost. By 1935, when the line had changed to the united front, the Rank-and-File Movement had been expelled from the Amalgamated and to help it form an independent union would have violated the new Moscow position. Indeed, after 1934, the trade union line of the Communist party meshed beautifully with the strategy of John L. Lewis. This meant, according to Lynd, that the rank-and-file dream passed into the hands of Lewis in the form of an organizing committee none of whose officers were steelworkers—an organizing committee which, in the words of Len DeCaux (1970, 280), a left-wing official of the early CIO, was "as totalitarian as any big business." The question remains, however, whatever the theoretical possibilities might have been, could the American Communist party, by then so highly bureaucratized and disciplined, surely, to borrow DeCaux's line, as totalitarian as any big business, and so tied to the COMINTERN for strategy and tactics, have ever built as militant a rank-and-file labor movement in steel as Lynd believes it could?

Even if the Communists could have demonstrated the creativity and flexibility necessary, would they have met with any greater enthusiasm among the steelworkers than SWOC apparently did? If the steelworkers were, as Lynd suggests, militant rank and filers, the answer is clearly yes. Other observers, however, have depicted the labor force as cautious and have suggested that deep sociocultural influences might have set the steel towns apart from other industrial environments. According to Clinton Golden and Harold Ruttenberg, the research director of SWOC, in their fascinating brief for labor-management cooperation, *The Dynamics of Industrial Democracy* (1942), the dominant social and cultural influences of the mine, mill, and factory towns had a far greater effect on the nature of workers' response than any other factors.

Golden and Ruttenberg argued that the turbulent labor situation in auto in contrast to the relatively peaceful situation in steel during the latter part of the 1930s demonstrated the degree to which union-management relations were influenced by social conditions. The more peaceful process in steel, they pointed out, occurred because of the settled nature of the steel towns. Two generations of steelworkers, sons and grandsons, made up the work force. They were fundamentally conservative and security conscious. The appeal of SWOC had to be that as a modern union it could establish collective bargaining peacefully, and organizers had to break down the fear that joining the union meant strikes.

Auto, by contrast, was a new industry, whose growth coincided with restrictive immigration to the United States. Almost half of Detroit's auto workers had migrated after the 1921 depression from other parts of the country. Thus the first generation of auto workers was still dominant, and the second and third overshadowed the first in steel. This continuity, according to Charles Walker in *Steeltown* (1950), probably also explains the strength of the employee representation plans and the decision of Little Steel to fight at a time when the CIO tide seemed unstoppable. Although most standard treatments concentrate on the skill with which SWOC captured the ERPs from within, little mention is made of the loyalty of a large number of steelworkers to their company unions. Brooks, in *As Steel Goes* (1940), grants that many ERPs were fairly effective and did not necessarily deserve the epithet of "company stooges." Galenson concurs and attributes the failure of the Little Steel strike in part to the loyalty of workers to the company unions and the success of the "back-to-work" movements in the steel towns.

Charles Walker demonstrates the basic conservatism of the steelworker communities and shows how that translated into relations in the mill in Elwood City, Pennsylvania (1950). According to Walker, the structure of the family and kinship system, along with proclivities for long-term economic planning and a high degree of home ownership, were basic to this conservatism. In Elwood City it was difficult to distinguish life inside and outside the mill. Practically all incumbents in top management jobs in the National Tube mill had risen from the ranks and had long service records. This was also true for a substantial percentage of all other employees. In October 1946, 50 percent of the mill population of 3,800 were thirty-eight years old or older, and 54 percent had more than ten years of service, 33 percent more than twenty years, and 15 percent more than twenty-five years. Seventy-eight percent were married, 51 percent owned their own homes, and a full 15 percent lived with their parents. Not surprisingly, Walker found that many of these workers thought that good industrial relations in the mill were the result of good and neighborly relations in the outside community and vice versa.

John Bodnar's study of immigrant steelworkers in Steelton, Pennsylvania (1977), supports what Walker found in Elwood City. Steelton's Slavic steelworkers were marked by a hard-headed realism and an emphasis on job security, which combined with the insulating effect of their familial and community ties. They ultimately became loyal union men, but they generally stayed on the sidelines during the great battles of the Little Steel strike.

These findings, skimpy as they are, hardly paint a picture of a militant rank and file ready to move spontaneously toward the syndicalism of the new left. Nor do they lend much support to the argument that the CIO was a mass social democratic movement. What they do suggest, however, is one of the themes that runs through the history of the United Steelworkers and the steel industry more than any other—the impulse toward labor-management cooperation.

A Theme of Labor-Management Cooperation

Whether one sees this trend toward labor-management cooperation as a confirmation of the new left analysis that labor was coopted and controlled by monopoly capitalism or as evidence that the movement was taking its first steps toward a type of worker codetermination similar to the social democratic solutions of West Germany or Sweden, there is little question that labor-management cooperation has been a hallmark of steel unionism from the beginning. Indeed, one can trace this strain back to pre-union days by noting the significance of welfare capitalism and company unionism in the industry. David Brody has shown that to interpret welfare capitalism and company unionism entirely, or even mainly, as nothing more than attempts to hoodwink workers into forgoing real power through unionism is to misinterpret badly their rationale and impact. I am concerned here, however, mainly with the union era. Murray himself advocated cooperation with industry in his book *Organized Labor and Production,* which he wrote while head of SWOC. Murray believed that strong, mature unions should share both profits and responsibility with industry: "As management and labor . . . become more nearly equal in bargaining power, they either wage war to gain the spoils of production restriction and scarcity prices, or they can together devise improved production practices that increase social income" (1940, 214). "Power," according to Murray, "could not be disassociated from responsibility" (page 214). If labor failed to develop an adequate sense of responsibility for productivity, bitterness and conflict would ensue, which would reduce the opportunity for constructive accommodation and the community of interest between management and the union. According to Murray, such cooperation would evolve when collective bargaining matured and "there would be a demand for labor leaders who are production conscious and who are ready and able to cooperate with management in furthering the common enterprise" (page 215).

Murray's vision of industrial democracy led the United Steelworkers to be primary proponents of the industrial councils idea during the war. Two of Murray's top lieutenants, Golden and Ruttenberg, in their book dedicated to Murray, *The Dynamics of Industrial Democracy* (1942), put forth the idea of mutual trusteeship between labor and management in chapters entitled "Paths to Industrial Peace," "Ways to Productive Efficiency," and "Means to Full Production and Employment." It was Murray and his aides who encouraged Steelworker staff representative Joseph Scanlon to develop what became the Scanlon Plan, the country's most durable labor-management cooperation program. Such faith in class collaboration and cooperation is not surprising in a man such as Murray, who, as a devout Roman Catholic, drew his labor ideology from the papal encyclicals *Quadragesimo Anno* and *Rerum Novarum.*

Indeed, the religious dimension of Murray's social and labor theory was evident in his support for the moral rearmament movement, a Protestant variant on Catholic social theory based on class love and global cooperation as an answer to communism. Steelworker staff representative John Riffe was the leading advocate for moral rearmament in the labor movement, and a theatrical show, the Moral Rearmament Review, was presented, with Murray's strong support, at the USWA convention in Cleveland in 1948.

Given Murray's orientation, it is also not surprising that labor-management cooperation has been a hallmark of labor relations in steel in the years since Murray died. Most recently, the union has supported the establishment of quality circles and other innovations with regard to union involvement in the decision-making process. Such cooperation was demonstrated before that in the joint labor-management human relations committees of Murray's successor, David J. McDonald, and in the famous Fairless tours when McDonald and Benjamin Fairless of U.S. Steel toured the mills together. McDonald bore the onus of these tours with those who were critical of his closeness to the leaders of the companies, but, in fact, they were planned before Murray's death. McDonald's successor, I. W. Abel, continued the tradition with the Experimental Negotiating Agreement (ENA) with Big Steel. In the Benjamin Fairless Memorial Lectures at Carnegie-Mellon University, Abel described the ENA as a cooperative effort between union and management to fight imports and end the costly practice of stockpiling before negotiations. In those lectures, President Abel referred to Murray's vision of union responsibility for the health of the industry as a justification for the ENA.

A word of caution is necessary here. We should be careful not to accept this picture of the rank and file in steel as conservative, cautious, loyal, and cooperative without coming to grips with the question of what happened to the militant workers of Homestead, during the strike of 1901, in McKeesport, and during the great steel strike of 1919.

Earlier in this chapter, I mentioned Brody's three historiographical categories for delineating the CIO. One remains to be dealt with—the CIO, and by implication the Steelworkers, as an extension of the pure and simple economic unionism of the AFL. Brody addresses this issue in his chapter, "The Origins of Modern Steel Unionism: The SWOC Era."

Why the Relative Neglect of the Steelworkers?

There is still the question of why the modern history of steel unionism has been relatively neglected by historians. It is certainly not because of their aversion to the industry. It is the rare labor historian who does not consider the attempts to organize the steel industry in the late nineteenth and early twentieth centuries as among the most significant events in labor history. Studies of Homestead in 1892, McKeesport in 1906, and the strikes of 1901 and 1919 abound. I cannot help but think that the lack of scholarly interest reflects more than anything the political persuasion of labor historians. The Steelworkers have probably disappointed historians. Labor relations in steel since the 1930s have generally been peaceful. The relationship has been characterized by pure and simple unionism, by collective bargaining gains rather than strikes. The Steelworkers are not alone in suffering from relative neglect. After all, there are a good deal more books and articles about the Industrial Workers of the World than about the AFL, although the imbalance hardly reflects the relative historical significance of the two organizations.

Another reason for the relative neglect of the Steelworkers might simply be that although fifty years seems like a long time in our terms, it is but a blink of an eye in historical time. Many historians would define any writing on an institution so young as current events rather than history. Youth, however, has not deterred scholars from a rather intense interest in the United Automobile Workers. Whatever the reasons, it is my hope that the imbalance will be redressed and that a new edifice of historical scholarship will emerge on this great union and its first president.

THE ORIGINS OF
MODERN STEEL UNIONISM:
THE SWOC ERA

David Brody

THERE has never been much dispute, either among contemporary observers or among historians, about the broad contours of the early history of industrial unionism. The movement began with a powerful burst of rank-and-file activity, fed by long-standing grievances and set in motion by the New Deal assertion of labor's right to organize and bargain collectively. The organizations that emerged were antibureaucratic, prone to direct action, and receptive to radical influences. The trade union history of the 1930s turns very largely on the capacity of the labor movement to contend with these rank-and-file impulses. The signal failure of the AFL on this score led directly to the creation of the Committee for Industrial Organization in 1935. The industrial unions fostered by the CIO both capitalized on and ultimately contained these rank-and-file energies, but at different rates and with varying institutional consequences. In a union such as the United Electrical, Radio and Machine Workers (UE), vestiges of the original rank-and-file character remain alive to this day. (See, for example, the account of the UE Convention in the *New York Times,* September 22, 1986.)

Steel unionism occupies the far opposite position on the spectrum. From the moment the CIO entered the industry in 1936, organizational development proceeded comparatively immune from the rank-and-file pressures agitating other industrial unions. While sitdowns and wildcat strikes swept the automobile industry, remarked steel union officials, "steelworkers in Pittsburgh,

Homestead, and other steel-producing towns made the transition from individual to collective bargaining with little, if any, strife" (Golden and Ruttenberg 1942, 110). Both in its internal operations and in its control over collective bargaining, SWOC was highly centralized, and so was the United Steelworkers of America which succeeded it in 1942. There was no factionalism, scarcely any dispute over union policy or political issues, and no challenges whatever to the national leadership—all in stark contrast, as Philip Taft (1956) remarked, to the turbulent history of the UAW. In their remarkable book *The Dynamics of Industrial Democracy*, two high-ranking officials of SWOC, Clinton S. Golden and Harold J. Ruttenberg, cogently express the vision of progressive labor relations—based on collective bargaining, labor-management cooperation, and national planning—which required a centralized union capable of acting with "responsibility and authority" (1942, xxi and 10).

The contrast between auto and steel drew much comment at the time. It was, Golden and Ruttenberg argued, a matter of "social environment." Auto was a new industry that had grown dramatically during the 1920s and that operated in bursts of seasonal activity. It attracted raw industrial recruits from America's hinterland. They came and went and "never got a chance really to settle down, to get a feeling of really 'belonging' in the auto towns." The Depression had hit the steelworkers equally hard, but they "bunched up and stuck close to their homes awaiting an upturn." Although they were also from rural backgrounds, they had arrived from Europe decades earlier and "through the generations acquired the industrial disciplines and a sense of 'belonging', if not to their steel towns at least to the parts dominated by their particular nationality group" (1942, 117). Moreover, a long and sobering experience with trade unionism had given the steelworkers a healthy respect for the power of their employers. With memories of the 1919 steel strike still fresh in their minds, they held back "until it was abundantly clear that SWOC would win in the end." Nor, once in, were they strike-prone. "A strike disrupts their community and personal lives so tremendously that, we have found, only the sharpest provocation will cause the men who make steel to take drastic action." They accepted "the orderly establishment of union-management relations at the outset of 1937," Golden and Ruttenberg concluded, "not because they were any better led or less bitterly opposed than auto workers, but because they were dominated by a social environment that had cast them into accustomed routines which they did not lightly upset" (page 112).

This analysis is worth pondering. Golden and Ruttenberg were drawing on extensive firsthand knowledge. Both had been involved with the steelworkers' movements in the Pittsburgh district many months before the arrival of the CIO, and both started on the ground floor with SWOC—Golden in charge of the Northeast district, Ruttenberg as national research director. The pickup social history they wrote, in addition, strikingly prefigures current historical scholarship on the 1930s. There is the same crucial assumption that patterns of collective action are linked to the community life and sociocultural characteristics of specific industrial populations. Some of these groups exhibited a persistent militancy, such as the French-Canadian carpet workers of Woonsocket, Rhode Island, and the West Coast seamen and longshoremen (Gerstle 1978, 161–67; Nelson 1984, 141–82). In the case of the Slavic steelworkers, however, their principal historian, John Bodnar, has argued that their ethnic characteristics inculcated a high degree of "realism" in the struggle for industrial justice (1977 and 1980). Limited expectations, the high premium they placed on job security, and the insulating effects of family and community ties produced just the restraint described in *The Dynamics of Industrial Democracy*. Likewise, its suggestions about the social sources of militancy among auto workers after 1936 are supported by recent studies of shop floor actions in auto and rubber, which stress their volatility, their "parochial and localistic focus," and, in the case of the Packard wildcat strike of 1943, even their racism (Nelson 1982; Lichtenstein 1980).

Yet, between 1933 and 1936, the labor upsurge in steel in fact conformed quite closely to the pattern for the mass-production industries in general. Strike activity in 1933–34 (as measured by the ratio of strikers to the total labor force) was of roughly the same intensity as in rubber and auto. In steel, the number of strikers jumped from nearly zero in 1932 to thirty-four thousand in 1933 (Peterson 1937, 124, 131, 148; Edwards 1984, 154). The feeble Amalgamated Association of Iron, Steel and Tin Workers

(AFL), which had fewer than 5,000 members in 1933 and virtually no organizing capacity, reported 129 new lodges and 50,000 members in February 1934. Membership figures, dubious at best because of record-keeping breakdowns at AAISTW headquarters, do not in any case capture the full scope of rank-and-file mobilization. Probably the best estimate is Clinton Golden's, who, after lengthy dealings with the AAISTW in early 1935, set the number of workers who had at least signed cards in the previous twenty months at perhaps 150,000, or one out of two in the basic industry (Brooks 1978, 141). Just as telling were the signs of interracial solidarity, which went counter to the traditional hostility between white and black steelworkers (10 percent of the labor force in 1933) (Cayton and Mitchell 1939, chap. 10). Further, a new spirit of independence manifested itself at the ballot box. Even in such closed company towns as Aliquippa, Pennsylvania, where Jones & Laughlin bosses boasted of their political control, steelworkers voted overwhelmingly Democratic from 1934 onward.

In steel, as elsewhere, the first organizational surge proved short-lived. The demands for action against open-shop employers—three-quarters of the steelworkers on strike in 1933–34 were fighting for union recognition—came up against the caution of the AFL leadership and the eagerness of the National Recovery Administration (NRA) for industrial peace. The result was futile compromise, which in steel took the form of the impotent Steel National Labor Relations Board, followed in the second half of 1934 by a precipitous decline in union membership. Those early struggles left in their wake local leaders and activists who kept skeleton organizations alive and continued the union struggle. These men had taken over the Amalgamated convention of April 1934, had led the abortive fight for union recognition in May and June, and thereafter had attempted unsuccessfully to wrest control of the Amalgamated from the old-line leadership. Activists such as Clarence Irwin of Youngstown, Ohio, and Albert Atallah of Aliquippa were still on the scene in early 1936 urging the CIO to enter steel.

Nor was the radical ingredient absent from the industry. As elsewhere, the sectarianism of the Third Period prevented the Communists from capitalizing on the labor unrest of the early

New Deal. The Steel and Metal Workers Industrial Union (SMWIU) registered some successes at the fringes of the industry but developed no mass following at the major centers. In 1934, however, with the shift to the united front, the SMWIU moved out of the industry (and in 1935, along with the parent Trade Union Unity League, dissolved) and directed its cadres to join the Amalgamated. There is some evidence of Communist influence within the steel rank-and-file movement from late 1934 onward (see, for example, Ruttenberg's notes, "Joint-district meeting of December 30, 1934"; Clarence Irwin to Ruttenberg, January 23, 1935; Ruttenberg to Heber Blankenhorn, March 28, 1935, all in Harold Ruttenberg Papers).

In one respect, the labor revolt in steel did diverge from the general pattern. The employee representation plans created to stymie Section 7(a) began to develop an increasing degree of independence. By the end of 1935, over the objections of management, a companywide ERP organization was crystallizing in U.S. Steel. In fact, in pleading the case for industrial unionism before the AFL Executive Council, John L. Lewis claimed he was much less concerned about rival radical unions than about a vigorous company-union movement (Minutes, April 30–May 7, 1935). There was, in any case, a keen sense of urgency about the steel situation within the newly formed CIO. *"Further delay may prove disastrous,"* warned the director of organization, John Brophy, in an assessment dated January 13, 1936 (Pollak 1936).

Some fifteen years ago, a new left school of labor history emerged that discovered in the turbulent 1930s the lost opportunity for a revolutionary labor movement, fueled, as George Rawick wrote in 1969, by "working-class self-activity . . . by struggle from below, by the natural organization of the working class, rather than by the bureaucratic elaboration of the administration of the working class from above" (1983, 147). The first serious effort at giving historical specificity to this formulation was a 1972 essay by Staughton Lynd in *Radical America* entitled "The Possibility of Radicalism in the Early 1930s: The Case of Steel" (Lynd 1983). Assessing the rank-and-file record I have just surveyed, Lynd did indeed find such possibility in steel. How are we to reconcile such drastically diverging conceptions of the militancy of the steelworkers as Lynd's and Golden and Ruttenberg's? We must first of all acknowledge the ideological imperatives: Golden and Ruttenberg were just as eager to show rank-and-file acquiescence in an industrial democracy based on industrywide bargaining and national planning as Lynd was to show a rank and file battling for his vision of a revolutionary industrial order. That both arguments should manage to be plausible says something about the complexity and elusiveness inherent in the study of popular movements.

Steelworkers were not homogeneous, any more than any other sector of the American working class. Everything we know about rank-and-file activists elsewhere who took on the burdens of industrial struggle during the 1930s tells us that they were, in one or more ways, an unrepresentative lot: they tended to be an elite in terms of skills and job status; at some point they had earlier been exposed to trade union or radical traditions; and their personal histories had somehow made them unusually sensitive to injustice, and willing to resist it (Brody 1985). The rank-and-file leaders in steel were no different.

> Almost all of us were middle-aged family men, well paid, and of Anglo-Saxon origin. Most of us were far better off than the average steel worker and didn't have much to gain ... except a certain amount of personal prestige. Almost all of us could have done better for ourselves if we had stuck with the companies and not bothered about the rest of the men. But for various reasons we didn't. We were sure that the mass of steel workers wanted industrial unionism, and so did we. (Brooks 1940, 46–47)

Nor, for the great majority outside the activist ranks, do either/or terms apply. The social environment of the steel towns could have inculcated the sense of "realism" of which John Bodnar writes without precluding outbursts of rebellion, triggered, for example, by the enunciation of Section 7(a), or by the sense of hope that exploded in the brief mass strike at Jones & Laughlin in May 1937 after the U.S. Steel agreement, or by the heady feeling of power in the wake of that victory, which brought on the tragic Little Steel strike.

We would do well to see the labor situation as it appeared to the founders of the CIO when they rebelled against AFL complacency in late 1935. The Wagner Act had recently been passed, the authority of employers was much eroded, the industrial workers were astir. Anything seemed possible, but nothing was certain. It took a very particular series of historical steps—three in number—to translate the possibilities of the winter of 1935–36 into the steel unionism celebrated by Golden and Ruttenberg in *The Dynamics of Industrial Democracy* six years later.

First was the creation of the instrument for organizing the industry. The labor movement had never seen the likes of the Steel Workers' Organizing Committee—not for the resources at its command, nor its immunity from constraining trade union rules and practices, nor the operational control vested in its leadership. One need only turn back to the National Committee for Organizing the Iron and Steelworkers, the unwieldy and weakly financed consortium of twenty-one national unions that ran the 1918–19 steel drive, to realize how revolutionary SWOC was in trade union terms. By the same token, we can only account for the establishment of SWOC by placing it in the trade union context of 1935–36.

It has become unfashionable to dwell on the institutional side of the industrial union struggle. But the CIO was, in the most direct sense, the product of disputes over jurisdictional rights, trade autonomy, and vested union interests within the AFL. Such issues also defined the terms of struggle for the rank-and-file movements in the field. It mattered enormously, as it happens, that no national unions existed at the start of the NRA period for auto or rubber, while iron and steel was under the jurisdiction of the Amalgamated—never mind that it was a nearly moribund and hopelessly outdated organization. In 1933–34, auto and rubber workers were channeled into AFL federal labor unions, while steelworkers went directly into the Amalgamated Association. (AFL President William Green would have preferred to place the steelworkers in federal labor unions, but he did not dare bypass the Amalgamated.) This difference, although it did not particularly affect the boom-and-bust cycle of the rank-and-file movements, did largely determine their institutional history. In auto and rubber, the focus of struggle was over autonomy from the AFL, first through national councils, then in 1934–35 in the demand for autonomous national unions. The issue of industrial unionism was deeply implicated in this battle, for the trump card of the craft unions was that only national unions—like themselves—could exercise jurisdictional rights. Industrial unionism was much less of a fighting issue in steel, however, because the Amalgamated actually claimed an industrial jurisdiction. The rank-and-file struggle there took the form of a dispiriting factional struggle for control of the Amalgamated.

The CIO thus faced quite different situations in these three industries in late 1935. In auto and rubber, fledgling national unions chartered by the AFL (but denied full industrial jurisdictions) were already in the field and effectively under the control of independent rank-and-file leadership. If the CIO hoped to organize these industries, it would have to operate through the United Auto Workers and the United Rubber Workers. In contrast, rank-and-file activists in steel lacked an institutional base, and the old-line Amalgamated leadership tenaciously held on to office. The CIO knew that it could not organize steel through the Amalgamated, but neither was it willing, at a time when its future ties to the AFL were uncertain, simply to ignore the jurisdictional rights of the Amalgamated. (Nearly six months, strange as it seems, were consumed in wooing that decrepit old union into the CIO camp.) The establishment of an organizing committee was the answer to the CIO's dilemma, enabling it at once to move expeditiously and (in trade union terms) legally. The charter for SWOC, such as it was, was a memorandum of agreement setting out the terms by which the Amalgamated authorized the CIO to undertake an organizing drive in steel. None of this would have much mattered, of course, had the CIO—or, rather, John L. Lewis—not attached special importance to the steel industry. For Lewis, the organization of steel was a prerequisite for the success of the Mine Workers in the captive mines, a vital interest that prompted Lewis to commit vast resources of the United Mine Workers of America, both men and money, to making SWOC a reality (and, incidentally, to beginning thereby the transformation of the CIO into a movement rival to the AFL).

With SWOC in place, the organizing phase—the second step—commenced. Had the workers risen up in June 1936, steel unionism might have taken a quite different turn. But there was nothing like the mass insurgencies that swept through rubber and auto in 1936 and early 1937. "Our first problem was to banish fear from the steel workers' minds," remarked the chairman of SWOC, Philip Murray (Harbison 1940, 30). This was the premise on which all of SWOC's early tactics rested. It meant, first of all, a minimalist direct approach. The SWOC organizers who fanned out into the steel towns carried the pledge that the steelworkers would not be called out on strike. No initiation fees were charged, nor, from November 1936 onward, dues collected. The organization building that did occur took the form of an infrastructure of activists who would come out into the open only at a later stage. Meanwhile, an indirect strategy was strongly pressed. SWOC staged well-publicized conferences of ethnic and black leaders who endorsed the CIO. In the weeks before the November elections, the campaign shifted almost wholly into the political arena. By thus linking itself to ethnic and New Deal attachments, SWOC made considerable headway with the steelworkers in their communities. Inside the mills, the main effort was to "capture" the company unions of U.S. Steel. This consisted of a two-pronged attack—first, in Golden's words, to keep the employee representatives "biting at the heels" of management with demands intended, alternatively, to expose company weakness or the futility of the ERPs; and, second, to develop an ERP following that would march into SWOC at the right moment.

The campaign was, altogether, brilliantly conceived. Its success was not calculated on, nor did it build, a vigorous rank-and-file organization. At the beginning of 1937, SWOC claimed 125,000 members. This was essentially a paper organization, a mountain of membership cards plus an indefinable reservoir of goodwill. With bad news, it might have gone up in a puff of smoke.

But the news was astonishingly good. On March 2, 1937, the Carnegie-Illinois Steel Corporation, the steel-producing subsidiary of U.S. Steel, signed a preliminary agreement recognizing SWOC as the bargaining agent for its members. Membership surged, lodges were put on a firm footing, dues collection resumed effective April 1, and initiation fees commenced effective May 1. Contractual relations began with all the U.S. Steel subsidiaries—agreements were signed specifying the terms of employment, including a formal grievance procedure—and were extended to eighty-one companies within a month. The effective unionization of steel dates from March 2, 1937.

Three weeks earlier in Flint, Michigan, sitdown strikers had forced General Motors to recognize the UAW. In Akron, Ohio, a year of strike action against the major rubber companies was still in process. On March 3, in fact, ten thousand Firestone workers began a fifty-nine-day strike for recognition. In steel, the decisive breakthrough occurred with no such rank-and-file struggle. It could not, indeed, have been more remote from the shop floor. Recognition stemmed from a series of secret meetings in Washington and New York City between the chairman of U.S. Steel, Myron P. Taylor, and John L. Lewis, to which no one in SWOC—not even Murray—was privy until the last minute. Not many events so completely shape the future of an institution as did the Taylor-Lewis agreement. Fewer still are accomplished with such clear-minded deliberation by the principal actors.

The CIO hailed Taylor's "industrial statesmanship." This consisted partly of a tough-minded assessment of the balance of forces at the height of the New Deal. (For assessments of Taylor's logic, all pretty much in agreement, see, for example, "It Happened in Steel," 1937; Galenson 1960, 93–96; and Dubofsky and Van Tine 1977, 272–77). U.S. Steel seemed unlikely to prevail in the long run and, more important, was not prepared (unlike the Little Steel firms) to bear the costs of seeing the game played out. But Taylor's "statesmanship" did not consist simply of bowing to the inevitable. Collective bargaining, if it was bound to come, could scarcely have taken a better form than that proffered by the CIO. For one thing, the captive mines agreement, dating back to 1933, had given U.S. Steel confidence in John L. Lewis and his practice of disciplined unionism. (Tom Moses, head of the Steel Corporation's coal operations, served as a close adviser to Taylor during the negotiations.) There was, moreover, a compelling economic logic. The industry's system of administered prices and (as a corollary) stabilized wages had broken down early in the Depression. The economic history of steel during the 1930s turns very much on its efforts to reconstruct a stabilized price-wage structure. U.S. Steel was no longer powerful enough to serve effectively as the price leader, nor, in the post-NRA years, was collusive pricing politically acceptable. As Lloyd Ulman asks, "If John Lewis could furnish the industry with a floor under wages, could one be certain that his demand for recognition was the knock of doom and not of opportunity?" (1961, 232).

The refusal of the Little Steel companies to follow U.S. Steel's lead kicked one of the props from under this logic. There would not be the industrywide bargaining favored by the CIO. But the practical effect of the Carnegie-Illinois agreement was the same. The wage advance and forty-hour week granted in March 1937 immediately became the industry standard. A general price increase quickly followed, which was, by the estimate of Marriner Eccles of the Federal Reserve Board, "greatly in excess of the rise that would be sufficient to compensate for the wage advance" (Bernstein 1970, 471). Mark here the precedent for the industry's postwar wage-price spiral.

The recession of 1937–38 further underscored the union's industrial role. Despite plummeting demand for steel, the union's contract was renewed in February 1938 without a wage cut. This was, asserted John L. Lewis, "a tribute to Mr. Taylor, not only as a leader of industry but as an American devoted to the furtherance of rational relationships and national stability." Myron Taylor, in fact, gravely doubted his firm's capacity to play that role under severe economic pressures—hence the escape clause attached to the new contract that gave either party the right to reopen it at any time. When steel prices broke in the summer of 1938, Philip Murray castigated the revival of cutthroat competition and warned that "if the steel corporations cannot put their own house in order," his union would seek "a constructive legislative program that will adequately protect the interests of the industry and its workers" (Harbison 1942, 530). The union itself lacked the economic muscle to prevent wage cuts in 1938, but in concert with the White House, it managed to bring so much political pressure to bear that U.S. Steel, despite wage chiseling by its competition, hesitated long enough in moving for reductions that the economy had time to revive in late 1938. (See *Steel Labor*, February 18, 1938, 2, and October 28, 1938, 1; SWOC Proceedings, Second Wage and Policy Conference, 1940, 8; and, for an invaluable account of the 1938 negotiations over the wage issue between U.S. Steel and the White House, McQuaid 1982, 11–17.) In retrospect (if not in the midst of the 1938 crisis), U.S. Steel could appreciate the effort SWOC had made to forestall the pressures of the marketplace. The union was a force to be relied on in the cause of industrial stability. It had been part of Myron Taylor's "statesmanship" to have perceived that truth when he voluntarily granted recognition to SWOC in March 1937. To that degree, Taylor deserves to be recorded among the shapers of modern steel unionism.

In the meantime, the power of state intervention began to bear on the organizing struggle in steel. It was a case against a steel company, Jones & Laughlin, that finally validated the constitutionality of the Wagner Act in April 1937. At issue was the dismissal of workers for union membership. The Court decision required Jones & Laughlin to reinstate them with back pay. This attack on the coercive powers of such recalcitrant employers as the Little Steel independents was of crucial importance in the union struggle and was used with devastating effect, for example, against Republic Steel, which was ordered to reinstate with full back wages several thousand workers who had been fired during the great 1937 strike. The key issue against U.S. Steel was a different unfair labor practice—company domination of employee organizations. SWOC had gained from the Taylor-Lewis agreement recognition only as bargaining agent *for its own members*. Carnegie-Illinois was free to negotiate with other agents and proceeded to do so with the ERP Pittsburgh District Council, which in January 1937 had purged itself of CIO sympathizers. After *Jones & Laughlin*, SWOC activated unfair-labor-practice charges on file against the ERPs as company-dominated organizations, and Carnegie-Illinois disestablished them by stipulation with the National Labor Relations Board (NLRB). SWOC thus gained a free field in representing the employees of Carnegie-Illinois and by the same legal process those of the other major firms as well. To achieve the bargaining rights contemplated by the law—NLRB certification as exclusive bargaining agent—involved a more drawn-out and legally complex struggle. This final step occurred at Jones & Laughlin right away; SWOC won consent elections at its two plants in May 1937. The other major independents held out until 1941. And SWOC did not gain exclusive bargaining rights at U.S. Steel subsidiaries until 1942.

The impact of the National Labor Relations Act in these early years should not be exaggerated. It served more as a register of the changing power balance than as the decisive determinant of the outcome. But the venue within which organizing was occurring had shifted. Increasingly, it fell within a legalistic framework of defined rights and formal procedures, and in so doing buttressed the kind of disciplined unionism SWOC was constructing.

No industry with steel's open-shop history could have been organized in the absence of massive rank-and-file mobilization. So strong was the response after the first U.S. Steel agreement that the national office had to plead with the lodges to avoid strike actions that might "result in the destruction of the Union. . . . For the sake of the future welfare of our Union and its members we urge all to remain at work pending our efforts to get the contracts signed in good faith" (Galenson 1960, 97). This first surge waned after the Little Steel defeat in the summer of 1937. A guerilla war for unionism then ensued inside the plants of the open-shop independents. As the shop steward system took hold and rank-and-file organization strengthened, lodges often gained de facto recognition and a form of shop floor bargaining that, in some ways, extended far beyond what would be permitted under a formal contract. The members-only recognition granted by U.S. Steel likewise placed the organizing burden on the rank and file. Only through the efforts of fellow workers could non-union workers be signed up and delinquent dues collected. The "dues picket lines" periodically thrown up at the plant gates were only the most visible sign of the day-to-day struggle to build up local organization.

This turmoil served, in fact, as a talking point for SWOC officials. If employers wanted labor peace, they would have to accept the union unreservedly: grant exclusive recognition and the union shop, check off union dues, and opt for arbitration as the final step in the grievance procedure. This measure of acceptance, said Golden, would "ensure the *responsibility* and *discipline* of the union" (Harbison 1940, 101). There is no question that Golden was right. In steel, the rank-and-file pressures could be contained. If employers did not deny it "power and status," SWOC was prepared "to be held responsible" (Cooke and Murray 1940, 187). This brings me to the third step in the shaping of steel unionism—the guiding leadership of one man, Philip Murray.

Murray was in many ways an unlikely figure for the role in which he was cast as chairman of SWOC. He had spent his mature career, since 1920, as vice president of the Mine Workers (a post from which he continued to draw his salary during the entire life of SWOC), the loyal subordinate of John L. Lewis in bad times as well as good. Murray was, by contrast to the imperious Lewis, an unremarkable man—plain-spoken, unassuming, most at home in the Pennsylvania coal towns in which he had grown up. The testimony of all who knew him was invariably to his decency and personal warmth. "It was Murray's special quality to touch the love and not the fear of men," wrote an admiring Murray Kempton (Bernstein 1970, 441). Within the emerging steel union, Murray was everywhere regarded with affection and reverence (even by those who grumbled about his policies). No one who knew Phil Murray could think of him as power-hungry. But, as chairman of SWOC, he in fact wielded extraordinary powers.

SWOC was a wholly anomalous trade union entity. It quickly assumed the character of a national union in scope and function but entirely lacked the constitutional base governing national unions. This ordinarily derives from the local unions, whose delegates in convention make constitutional rules and national policies and who remain (notwithstanding the powers they grant to the national executive) the ultimate source of authority. SWOC's authority derived not from below but from a memorandum of agreement by which the legally constituted national union in the industry—the inactive Amalgamated Association—authorized the CIO to set up an organizing committee with "power to handle all matters relative to the organizing campaign, other than the issuance of [lodge] charters" (which the Amalgamated would grant) and "exclusive power to deal with the steel companies in order to reach agreements" (except for existing Amalgamated contracts). No provision was made for internal governance except that the chairman of the CIO would appoint a "policy committee" (which was, in a formal sense, SWOC) whose meetings would occur "at the call of the [SWOC] chairman as conditions and circumstances warrant" (Bernstein 1970, 440–41). Half drawn from other CIO unions, half from SWOC functionaries, the committee met infrequently and only to ratify the actions of the chairman. It in no way controlled him.

As an appointee of the CIO, Murray was formally subject to

the direction of John L. Lewis. But after that first intervention to gain recognition from U.S. Steel, Lewis by choice left Murray pretty much on his own, and increasingly, as SWOC became stronger, the choice was no longer Lewis's. With Murray's accession to the presidency of the CIO in 1940, he became quite literally his own boss. No leader of a national union ever had so unlimited an authority as Murray did as chairman of SWOC.

There was never any question about how Murray would use his authority. As the first policy statement asserted, SWOC "will insist on a centralized and responsible control of the organizing campaign . . . and will insist that local policies conform to the national plan of action upon which it decides. . . . Responsibility begins and ends with this Committee" (Sweeney 1956, 12–13). There was, in Murray's mind, no separating the campaign phase which called forth so strong an insistence on centralized control from the union-building phase which would follow. It was too soon for the steelworkers to run their own union, Murray kept insisting. "We are an infant, so to speak, from the standpoint of age" (Ulman 1962, 6), he told the delegates to the 1940 policy convention.

Murray's paternalism always allowed for forms of participation. After the preliminary U.S. Steel agreement of March 2, 1937, he gathered representatives from all the Carnegie-Illinois lodges "for the purpose of preparing . . . proposals" for negotiating the final contract. Out of this meeting evolved the wage policy committee, made up of all local presidents, which took part in U.S. Steel contract negotiations (a second committee was created for the Little Steel companies in 1941). Actual bargaining, however, remained wholly in the hands of SWOC officials: the wage policy committee served as an authorizing agency in advance and a ratifying agency afterward. Likewise, on two occasions, in 1937 and in 1940, Murray called "wage and policy" conventions. These were specifically confined to the consideration of negotiation policy and rules governing the local lodges (the term *lodges* was a carryover from Amalgamated usage but was later dropped). It was not clear, within those limits, whether their resolutions could have binding power on SWOC officers. The issue was, however, moot. The conventions merely authorized SWOC negotiators to do their best in the forthcoming round and otherwise approved rules already in place or that the officers of SWOC wanted put in place.

The contours of a national union gradually emerged under Murray's firm hand. Borrowing from the Mine Workers, SWOC adopted a geographical structure of regions and districts. All the directors were appointed by the chairman of SWOC and served at his pleasure. The same was true of the large field staff (so that, among other things, the numerous Communists who had been hired could be used and then discarded when they became troublesome). The national office likewise controlled the finances: the lodges sent in monies collected and in turn received a specified portion back; they were not permitted to deviate from standard dues and initiation fees (one dollar and three dollars respectively) without the approval of the national office. No strikes could be called without national permission. SWOC officials negotiated and signed all contracts. These included grievance procedures that required the entry of a SWOC representative at the fourth step, thereby denying to the lodges the decision of whether to go to arbitration at the fifth step or to retain the option of striking. Strikes in violation of the contract were dealt with sternly, if need be by expelling the troublemakers. It was a sad reality, remarked Golden and Ruttenberg (1942, 58), that "most militant local union leaders, who rise to the surface in the organizing stage of unions, fall by the side when the union moves into the stage of constructive relations with management."

The transition from organizing committee to national union in May 1942 gave constitutional legitimacy to these institutional developments. The only substantial departures involved the popular election (rather than appointment) of the district directors and the creation of an executive board (on which all district directors served) with substantial powers. Otherwise, the new United Steelworkers of America carried over quite intact the forms and practices of SWOC. (For a thorough analysis of this institutional history, see Ulman 1962.)

Philip Murray built the steel union in service to his particular vision of industrial democracy. This derived, most directly, from his long association with the Mine Workers, which provided him (and the many other UMWA people in SWOC) not only with an institutional model but also with an appreciation for union discipline, fully empowered, seasoned leadership, and constructive labor-management relations based on industrywide bargaining. A devout Catholic, Murray was deeply influenced by the concept of the just industrial order in Leo XIII's encyclical *Rerum Novarum* (1891) and, as an equally ardent New Dealer, by the promise of national planning. In the winter of 1940–41, these ideas crystallized into Murray's proposal for industrial councils, in which labor and management would be equally represented, to run defense industry under the aegis of the state. During the war, the steel union advocated "a program of national democratic planning—a program designed to translate the full production and employment of the war effort into full production and employment in the manufacturing of peacetime goods" (USWA Proceedings, First Constitutional Convention, 74; for Murray's industrial councils plan, see *Steel Labor,* January 31, 1941, 2, and April 18, 1941, 11).

Murray's vision never, of course, came to pass, not during the war, and not in the reaction that followed. And this brings me to my final point. We are speaking of beginnings. If it was not in Philip Murray's hands to realize his vision of industrial democracy, neither was it in the hands of the union he built to control its future. Powerful political and market forces have acted on—and continue to act on—the course of trade unionism in the steel industry. Differences among industrial unions, large as they seemed at the start, shrink in the perspective of the common history they have since shared. Yet beginnings do matter. It remains the historian's task to work out to what degree, and in what ways, the SWOC years determined the next half-century of trade union history of the American steel industry.

LABOR'S ODD COUPLE: PHILIP MURRAY AND JOHN L. LEWIS

Melvyn Dubofsky

FOR more than twenty years the lives and careers of Philip Murray and John L. Lewis were closely intertwined. Both men made their marks first as leaders in the coal miners' union, the United Mine Workers of America, then as the promoters of an insurgent movement within the AFL in 1934 and 1935, and finally as the first and second presidents of the CIO. More often than not during that time, Murray served as Lewis's loyal lieutenant in the UMW and the CIO. Lewis made policy; Murray implemented it. Lewis dominated the public scene; Murray moved more furtively in the labor giant's shadow. Lewis left shattered individuals, friendships, and alliances in his trail; Murray tried to pick up the pieces. Throughout their long working relationship, Murray never openly questioned or challenged Lewis, until, that is, the rupture of their personal and institutional association in 1941–42.

Yet it would have been hard to find two men more dissimilar in demeanor, character, personal beliefs, and styles of private and public behavior. Lewis was imperious. Murray was more egalitarian. Lewis had few loyalties outside his family. Murray proved extremely loyal to friends, union associates, and political allies, as well as kin. Lewis lived in a regal style, catered to by personal servants; dressed in the finest custom-made clothes; and resided in a suburban home crammed with rare and valuable antiques. Murray lived modestly in a respectable but nondescript residential neighborhood of Pittsburgh even after he had obtained the substantial salary and perquisites that accompanied high trade union office. Lewis vacationed in the haunts of the rich on the Florida Gulf Coast, around Jackson Hole, Wyoming, and on the European continent. Murray usually remained at home or relaxed in places where ordinary workers felt comfortable. Lewis had no firm or fixed religious beliefs and never attended church. Murray was a devout Roman Catholic who attended mass regularly and sought to incorporate forms of social Christianity into the practice of trade unionism. Lewis declined to associate with fellow trade unionists or ordinary workers; he preferred the company of businessmen, high public officials, and the socially eminent. Murray felt more at home among union brothers and coal miners. Lewis abstained from alcohol; Murray enjoyed sharing a round or two with the boys at the neighborhood tavern. Such contrasting styles defined Lewis and Murray as the American labor movement's odd couple.

For more than twenty years the obviously different public and private personas of Murray and Lewis, as such close associates as Len DeCaux (1970, 391–402, passim), Lee Pressman (1958, 193–206, passim), and Harold Ruttenberg (1942, 23–26), pointedly noted, served well the purposes of both men. (See also Bernstein 1969, 447.) Murray's deep religiosity and conviviality with workers provided the UMW with links to the everyday culture of its rank and file that the distant Lewis could not. Murray could sell Lewis's policies to the coal miners on a man-to-man basis, extremely important among a group of workers with an exaggerated sense of manliness. By contrast, Lewis operated more effectively in carrying the union's case before corporate executives, public officials, and the media barons, among whom he felt no sense of inferiority. In other words, Murray was a trade union leader drawn directly from the ranks, never far from the union rank and file in his style and behavior, and a perfect exemplar of the working-class leader who never forgot his roots. Lewis, however, acted as the trade union counterpart of the corporate executive; he issued orders to subordinates, disciplined the insolent, and discharged the rebellious. Whatever his social roots, Lewis traveled in a milieu of executive washrooms, conference rooms, and dining rooms, and he occupied a presidential office that the journalist Marquis Childs (1958,

60–61) described as "a great office [in which] . . . you waded through the rug a couple of miles and got over to the great man."

Lee Pressman, who worked first for Lewis and then for Murray in the CIO, explained the differences between the two labor leaders by saying of Murray: "Murray never did enjoy sitting and talking with the so-called great. He always felt much better going back to the homely people, and getting the feeling of knowing what was going on in the mines, with the guys back home. It wasn't just a show with him. He actually felt refreshed when he did that" (1958, 183–84). This approach was acceptable to Lewis as long as Murray loyally implemented his commander's policies among the troops. When loyalty to Lewis conflicted with Murray's devotion to his own personal, union, and political faiths, as happened in 1941–42, the two labor leaders experienced a personal and institutional rift that neither time nor memory would ever heal. How and why John L. Lewis and Philip Murray, labor's odd couple, came to a parting of the ways is the focus of the rest of this paper.

Men of Similar Backgrounds

Both Murray and Lewis traced their family roots to the Celtic fringe of England. Lewis, who was born in Iowa in 1880, was descended from a line of Welsh small-land holders and coal miners. Murray, who was born in Blantyre, Scotland, in 1886, came to the United States with his Irish-born father on Christmas Day 1902. By then, the adolescent Murray was already a coal miner and union member, a craft he had learned from his father in the collieries of Scotland, which filled in the late nineteenth century with desperately poor Irish immigrants. As the oldest male child in a family of thirteen, Phil went to work in the mines at the age of ten and contributed his wages to the family budget. Like many other miners of their era, Phil and his father reacted to the demand for skilled mine labor in the United States as well as the promise of steadier work and higher wages. They joined a younger brother of Philip's, who had previously settled in Westmoreland County in the southwestern corner of Pennsylvania. After a year of working in the mines there, the three Murray men had reached their goal of earning enough money to bring the remainder of the family to the United States. (For more on Lewis's early life and career, see Dubofsky and Van Tine 1977, chap. 1; for more on Murray, see Schatz 1987, 235–40, and Bernstein 1969, 441–47.)

As a young man working in the nonunion mines of western Pennsylvania, Murray quickly learned how helpless the individual miner was compared to management. The victim of job inequities and a failed strike, Murray concluded that only a union could protect miners against victimization. "A coal miner has no money," he later recalled. "He is alone. He has no organization to defend him. He has nowhere to go. . . . The individual cannot protect himself because he has no organization. He has no one to go to" (Schatz 1987, 236). Murray determined to change that reality. He joined the United Mine Workers of America and by 1905 (before he was twenty) served as president of the union local in the village of Horning. At the same time, Murray took courses from the Scranton Correspondence School, an institution created to serve the anthracite miners of northeastern Pennsylvania who wanted to learn enough mathematics and science to rise to supervisory positions in the mines. Already a skilled miner, a local union president, and a partly educated man, all by the age of twenty-five, Murray married the daughter of a coal miner in 1910.

Lewis's life followed a similar trajectory in those years. He too joined his father in the mines as a teenager. But being in the farm state of Iowa, the Lewis men combined coal mining with farming. Like Murray, Lewis served as a local union official, in his case, in Chariton, Iowa, in 1900–01. For five years after that, however, Lewis rejected mining and unionism and instead drifted around the Rocky Mountain states before returning to Lucas, Iowa, where he tried his hand at business, politics, and theater. Lewis took a wife, the daughter of a local doctor, in 1908. Shortly thereafter the entire Lewis family moved to Panama, Illinois, in the heart of that state's coal fields, where Lewis dedicated himself to building a career in the labor movement.

Murray and Lewis found themselves in two of the most rapidly growing and contentious districts of the UMW, 5 in western Pennsylvania and 12 in Illinois. Both men lost no time in impressing higher officials in the UMW. Lewis used his connections with international officers to wangle himself an appointment as a full-time organizer on the staff of the American Federation of Labor. In that capacity, Lewis traveled around western Pennsylvania, northern West Virginia, and southeastern Ohio, where he heard much about a talented, attractive, young Scots-Irish union man in District 5, about whom John Brophy, president of District 2, heard it said that "he got along with people very well, because he was friendly and conciliatory rather than arbitrary. He was very likeable, and he's probably on his way up in mine workers' affairs" (Brophy 1964, 137).

Brophy proved accurate and also prophetic. In 1912 the president of the UMW, John White, appointed Murray to a vacant position on the International Executive Board, and three years later, in 1915, White and Lewis maneuvered Murray into the presidency of District 5. In 1917 John White went to work for the Wilson administration's Fuel Administration, his vice president succeeded to the presidency, and John L. Lewis moved into the vice presidency. Murray was among the district presidents who backed Lewis's rise in the union. Two years later, in 1919, Murray played a similar role in Lewis's appointment as acting president of the UMW. Murray urged fellow union officers to realize "that Lewis was a strong, able man, that he would really make something out of the United Mine Workers and that Frank Hayes [the president] was a well-meaning incompetent" (Brophy 1964, 150; Schatz 1987, 238). In January 1920 Lewis took over as acting president of the UMW, a position he obtained once again without winning an election for international union office, and, as one of his first acts, he appointed Murray as his vice president. At the age of thirty-three, Murray served as the second-ranking officer of the largest union in North America and as the loyal lieutenant of a man six years his senior.

Commander Lewis, Lieutenant Murray

For the next twenty years, Murray served Lewis with absolute, unswerving loyalty. Every crisis within the union and between the union and mine operators (or the government) found Murray at Lewis's side. The first test of Lewis's mettle as leader of the UMW came in the 1919 bituminous strike. When Lewis called the strike off at the behest of President Woodrow Wilson rather than risk outright federal repression, many among the rank and file and even some union officers rebelled. At the 1920 union convention, the dissidents took the offensive against Lewis. Murray, however, minced no words in defending his superior. Using almost the same words that Lewis had chosen to defend his decision to call the miners back to work in 1919, Murray told the convention delegates:

> When I made the motion that . . . we endorse the policy they have pursued, I did it with the feeling deep in my heart that it was the only course for the coal miners of this country to pursue under present day circumstances. There isn't a delegate in this convention who wants to . . . array the forces of his local union against the most powerful and strongly organized government in the world. (UMW Proceedings, 24)

When such district leaders as Alex Howat of Kansas, Frank Farrington of Illinois, and John Brophy of central Pennsylvania questioned or challenged Lewis's policies, Murray had a ready riposte. Like Lewis, Murray repudiated Howat's espousal of district autonomy and derided the Kansan's appeal to principles of trade union democracy. Murray never questioned Lewis's drive to centralize all power in the international office by diluting district autonomy and rank-and-file participation in union affairs. Murray also joined his leader in condemning the socialists and radicals within the UMW. He wanted no part of John Brophy's campaign to nationalize the coal mines and democratize the union, or even to organize the nonunion mines. A private letter from Murray to Lewis written on March 15, 1923 (UMW Archives) when the latter was visiting Great Britain on holiday, disclosed Murray's feelings. "Your close-up of British nationalization," he advised Lewis, "will give you an appreciation of the *nuts* who are leading the movement for nationalization on this side of the ocean" (emphasis added).

Thus Murray shared Lewis's desire to purge such "nuts" of any influence in the UMW. As Lewis drove first Howat, then Brophy, and finally Farrington out of the union, Murray cheered. Not once did he demur as Lewis increasingly concentrated power in the office of union president and eliminated the influence of

district officials and rank-and-file miners, whose contributions
had once made the UMW an especially democratic and militant
union. In the same letter in which he referred to union "nuts,"
Murray explained how he and Lewis conceived of administering
the UMW. Our constitutional departments, joshed Murray, "have
been making rulings having for their purpose the preservation
of the principles as laid down by yourself. It goes without saying
that these rulings not only protect the interests of the organization, but also protect our friends." Murray assured his boss
that "if any of these district officers peep their heads up, I will
do just as you would do,—kick them out of the organization,
then revoke their charters."

By 1928 Lewis and Murray had indeed won firm, uncontested
control of the UMW. All the challengers to their authority had
either been driven out of the union or had joined the Lewis team.
Yet the two UMW leaders found themselves rulers of a bankrupt
union empire. Everywhere they looked, with the exception of
District 12 in Illinois, their union lay in ruins. And nowhere was
the situation worse than in Murray's old District 5 in western
Pennsylvania, where mine operators had broken their agreements with the union and begun open-shop production. All the
policies Lewis and Murray had pursued—long-term no-strike
contracts with cooperative employers; good relations with Republican officials in Washington, especially Secretary of Commerce Herbert Hoover; and, finally, the policy of "no backward
step"—had failed to retard the union's decline. By 1930 even
District 12 was in the throes of collapse, in no small measure as
a result of Lewis's effort to obtain absolute control of the district
organization, a goal Murray shared.

Need for a National Policy

The rapid decline of their union in the 1920s prompted Lewis
and Murray to turn to the state for help. The two union leaders
now believed that only a national policy that eliminated cutthroat
competition in soft-coal mining, legitimated union recognition
as public policy, and mandated collective bargaining could save
their union from catastrophe. As Murray told the secretaries of
labor and commerce at the UMW conference on July 14, 1931:

"A start ought to be made somewhere and where ought we to go if not to our own Government to ask assistance in the situation" (see transcript, Department of Labor, Record Group 280, National Archives). The UMW had been trying to do just that since 1924, when Lewis had negotiated the Jacksonville Agreement with northern mine operators through the good offices of Herbert Hoover. The agreement, between the union and employers, prohibited strikes, lockouts, and changes in wages and working conditions during the term of three years. When the agreement began to collapse, Lewis turned to Hoover to save it. Unable to salvage the situation through administrative action, Lewis and Murray sought to achieve their goals through congressional legislation at the end of the Coolidge administration and the start of the Hoover administration. But the leaders of the Republican party resolutely refused to come to the aid of the UMW.

Throughout the prosperity decade of the 1920s, Lewis and Murray had been Republicans by convenience. Lewis, for one, had no firm political loyalties. Because the Republicans had full control of the national state during the 1920s and Lewis thought he could work with Hoover, he acted as that decade's leading labor Republican. Murray behaved similarly. He had registered as a Republican in Pennsylvania, an act David McDonald described (1969, 67) as being "a simple political necessity—like being a Democrat in Alabama."

Murray and Lewis grew disillusioned with the Republicans at about the same time, although Murray made the break sooner and more openly. In 1928, Lewis was chair of the Republican party's National Labor Committee and endorsed the election of Hoover, while Murray quietly supported Democrat Al Smith, a fellow Roman Catholic of Irish immigrant origins known to be sympathetic to workers and labor. Four years later, in the summer of 1932, Lewis was still chair of the Labor Committee when Murray led a six-man UMW delegation to Albany, New York, to meet with the Democratic presidential candidate, Franklin Delano Roosevelt. This action suggested neither a rift between Murray and Lewis nor any dissension within the UMW. Murray and his fellow delegates were undoubtedly serving the political interests of the UMW president, who had decided to support Roosevelt's election. Nonetheless, Murray's visit to Albany was to begin a relationship with Roosevelt that would ultimately drive a wedge between Murray and Lewis. Murray had found a friend and a political party to whom he would remain loyal for the remainder of his life. As Murray said in 1936 at the height of Roosevelt's popularity among coal miners, in one day labor had found a friend. "He was sitting on the end of a divan in his library in the Executive Mansion in Albany. . . . He knew the miners and their problems, and he said he would help them. Another day he was found sitting at a desk in the White House, and he said: 'I will help you by giving you the means of helping yourself.'" Roosevelt did not mislead the miners, remembered Murray (Schatz 1987, 244–45, and Dubofsky and Van Tine 1977, 177–78). And so, by 1936, the coal miner "shouted the name of Roosevelt as loudly as he shouted the words United Mine Workers" (Schatz 1987, 245). Or, as a West Virginia coal miner sang:

> *Some people don't know who to thank,*
> *for this "State of McDowell" that's so free;*
> *Give part of the praise to John Lewis*
> *and the rest of it to Franklin D.*
> (Korson 1965, 305)

Rebuilding the UMW

Largely because of the assistance of Roosevelt and the New Deal, Lewis and Murray succeeded in rebuilding the UMW in 1933 and 1934. Not only did they resurrect the union in its former strongholds in the Central Competitive Field; they also penetrated the anti-union bastions of southern Appalachia and the captive coal mines. By the end of 1934 the UMW was once again one of the nation's largest and most influential trade unions. Indeed, no labor organization and its leaders appeared to have greater influence in Washington, especially in the White House. Lewis and Murray sought to use that influence to organize workers throughout American industry, particularly in sectors theretofore impermeable to unions. "Without question," the UMW's leaders reported to their 1934 convention, "the problem of organizing the workers in . . . automobile, steel, rubber, lumber, electric, and other industries is of paramount importance to American labor. There is imperative necessity by the American Federation of Labor of a sound and practical policy that will meet the requirements of modern industrial conditions" (Proceedings, 56).

For the next year and a half Lewis sought to guide the AFL in this direction. But when his fellow vice presidents on the AFL Executive Council refused to accept his directives and the 1935 convention of the AFL rejected his strategy for unionizing mass-production workers, Lewis, in November 1935, founded the Committee for Industrial Organization. Two months later, in January 1936, at the UMW convention, Lewis and Murray vented their rage at the AFL, especially toward its president and their former union brother, William Green. "The sooner we get the hell away from them [the AFL] the better it will be for us," proclaimed Murray (Proceedings, 164). "The feeling of the crowd [UMW delegates] toward the A.F. of L.," noted Sidney Hillman, a CIO founder, to Charles P. Howard, secretary of the CIO, "is very bitter" (Hillman Papers, CIO folder). Shortly after the UMW convention adjourned, Lewis's economic adviser, W. Jett Lauck, recorded in his diary for February 3, 1936 (Lauck Papers): "Very dramatic scene. Green ruthlessly obliterated." And the man who had fought tenaciously against Lewis and Murray's influence in the UMW during the 1920s, John Brophy, wrote about the 1936 miners' convention (February 13, 1936): "I have never been as proud of my membership in the miners' union as I was during the convention. True, it wasn't absolute perfection, but as compared with any other group in the country today it was a beacon of light for the workers and those who value the democratic political structure" (Germer Papers, Box 2).

Always the Steadfast Servant

Throughout the early years of the CIO Murray steadfastly served Lewis precisely as he had during the previous sixteen years as vice president of the UMW. When Lewis appointed Murray as director of the CIO's campaign to organize the steelworkers, Murray pursued the policies of his long-time superior. Told to subordinate unionizing among steelworkers in the summer and fall of 1936 to the more important job of reelecting President

Roosevelt, Murray did precisely that. Although he was the putative director of SWOC, he remained silent and deferential throughout the negotiations between Lewis and Myron Taylor that led in March 1937 to the contract in which U.S. Steel recognized SWOC as the bargaining agent for its members. Murray signed the document the others had negotiated.

Whatever Lewis asked, Murray did. When the United Automobile Workers split into hostile factions in 1938, Lewis dispatched Murray and Hillman to repair the damage. Throughout the long and tedious negotiations between committees from the AFL and CIO authorized to heal the rift in the labor movement, Murray endorsed without qualifications all of Lewis's terms for peace. He expressed succinctly what he understood as Lewis's rationale for the formation and activities of the CIO. "Not a single member of this Committee [CIO] wants a split," Lewis said. "The C.I.O. was formed in desperation because there was no room for expansion under prevailing policies" (Ellickson Papers, Notes, CIO Executive Board meeting, November 7–8, 1936, 3–5). When the provisional committee transformed itself into the Congress of Industrial Organizations at a constitutional convention in Pittsburgh in 1938, Murray gladly consented to serve as one of President John L. Lewis's two vice presidents. This led many to perceive the CIO as simply the UMW in disguise.

Mounting Differences

During this same period, from 1936 through 1940, the ties that had bound Murray so tightly to Lewis were attenuating. Apparently Murray was irked because he had been excluded from the negotiations between Lewis and Taylor that culminated in the SWOC–U.S. Steel contract. Who can say what went on in Murray's mind, Lee Pressman later reminisced (1958, 193), when "the Myron Taylors didn't come to Phil Murray, but they went to John Lewis. . . . It is the kind of thing a man doesn't talk about, to any intimate." And when Murray took his first truly decisive action as head of SWOC, calling out the employees of the Little Steel companies in May 1937, he suffered a severe setback. Urged on by rank-and-file militants eager to strike against intransigent anti-union employers, Murray, in Pressman's words, "sent the men out to prepare for it. And he walked into it. And we took a terrific drubbing on that Little Steel Strike—a terrific drubbing" (page 194). Moreover, Murray had not cleared the strike with Lewis. Even if Lewis never criticized his subordinate publicly, more than likely he told Murray, "Phil, I don't know whether you should have done that. I don't know why you didn't check with me" (page 206). That from the man who had not cleared his decision to negotiate with Myron Taylor with the director of SWOC.

Political differences aggravated the emerging rift between Murray and Lewis. By 1937 the former had become a devoted loyalist of Roosevelt and the New Deal, and Murray was a man who believed in commitments. Lewis, by contrast, was growing estranged from Roosevelt, who, the CIO leader believed, was not according labor its just rewards and was dragging the United States into the maelstrom of European power politics. The more critical Lewis grew of the president the more firmly Murray supported Roosevelt. Ever the opportunistic politician, Roosevelt drew Murray (and also Hillman) more closely into White House and Democratic party networks while excluding Lewis. And as Lewis criticized Roosevelt's foreign policies, Murray warmly applauded American diplomatic participation in the antifascist coalition as defined by the president. The election of 1940 disclosed how far apart Murray and Lewis had drifted. The CIO chief participated prominently in most of the anti-Roosevelt political maneuvering and eventually even endorsed the Republican candidate for president, Wendell Willkie. Murray, most other CIO officers, and a clear majority of UMW members remained loyal to Roosevelt (indeed, in 1940, as a result of Lewis's political tactics, Murray received more nominations for UMW president from local unions than Lewis did). Roosevelt's reelection resulted in Lewis's last act of beneficence to his formerly loyal lieutenant and ultimately sealed their rupture.

Lewis had promised to resign as president of the CIO if Roosevelt was reelected, and he intended to implement that promise at the November 1940 convention of the CIO in Atlantic City. Lewis also intended to anoint Murray his heir apparent. Murray, however, had doubts about whether he should accept the presidency of the CIO. For too long he had acted in a subservient capacity to Lewis, and Murray did not know if he could change his style of behavior or if Lewis would tolerate such a change. According to Pressman, Murray "went through the pangs of hell, because he knew that Lewis was putting him there . . . expecting him to act as an agent for Lewis . . . And Murray was . . . trying to ask himself . . . was he going to be a man in his own right, or not?" (page 198). Murray saw no choice but to accept the nomination for the presidency. Yet, in his acceptance speech after his election, he expressed his anxieties openly. "I think I am a man," Murray remarked. "I think I have convictions, I think I have a soul and a heart and a mind. . . . With the exception, of course, of my soul, they all belong to me, every one of them" (CIO Proceedings 1940, 274).

At first, Lewis tried to enable Murray to be his own man. The UMW president steered clear of CIO business. Murray never challenged or criticized Lewis openly. Yet Murray grew increasingly uncomfortable in his dual role as president of the CIO and vice president of the UMW. He seemed fearful that leaving his office in the Miners' Building to work at CIO headquarters would sever his relationship with the UMW. "It became almost like a Freudian symbol," remembered Pressman, "the act of leaving there to go over to the C.I.O. building" (1958, 199).

Increasingly sensitive, Murray began to interpret Lewis's acts and words as personal rebukes. His perceptions were intensified by associates eager to curry favor with the new CIO president. Simultaneously, Murray's niece and Lewis's daughter, Kathryn, engaged in a virulent personal feud. Lewis, meantime, persisted in his criticism of Franklin D. Roosevelt's domestic and foreign policies. By contrast, the CIO, Murray included, was firmly committed to all of Roosevelt's policies, and the president had no more loyal constituency. In one last effort to heal their relationship, Lewis and Murray met in Atlantic City in mid-October 1941. Each man came away from the meeting with different recollections of what was said and had happened. Murray reported to Lee Pressman that Lewis pleaded with the CIO president not to endorse Roosevelt's foreign policy. Murray replied that he would follow the dictates of his own conscience even if it meant a final parting from Lewis (see Pressman 1958, 324–25).

The two labor leaders maintained a distant but cordial relationship until January 1942, when Lewis proposed a new peace plan that would remove Murray from a top leadership position and reunite the divided labor movement. Not having been consulted by Lewis about the peace plan, Murray responded angrily. "No one has a right to trade me for a job," he stressed. "My manhood requires a little reciprocity—and, by God, despite this feeble frame of mine, I will fight any living man to maintain my manhood." A little later, in a cold and curt official reply to Lewis addressed to "Dear Sir and Brother," Murray announced emphatically that all arrangements on behalf of unity "will necessarily have to be initiated through the office of the President of the Congress of Industrial Organizations" (*UMW Journal*, February 1, 1942, 6).

Relations Degenerate

Relations between the two men now degenerated into open war. The *UMW Journal* repeatedly lambasted Murray and his fellow officers of the CIO as lackeys of Roosevelt. Lewis compelled Murray to choose between his responsibilities as president of the CIO and his obligations as an officer of the UMW. The UMW engaged in a series of jurisdictional conflicts with CIO affiliates, and Lewis demanded that the CIO repay its enormous financial debt to the miners' union. When Murray defended the interests of the CIO, Lewis's agents charged the former with treason to the UMW. Finally, in May 1942, Murray announced that he would yield to "no dictator in or out of the labor movement." Realizing that his days with the UMW were numbered, Murray on May 22 accepted the salaried presidency of the United Steelworkers of America (see the *New York Times*, May 3, 1942, 2, and May 4, 1942, 8).

The following Monday, May 25, Murray entered the basement conference room of the UMW, a chamber dedicated to the influence and power of Lewis, to confront fellow members of the UMW's policy committee and executive council. Murray defended his policies as president of the CIO quietly and almost deferentially. Lewis criticized Murray for neglecting the welfare of the UMW and for dual loyalty, as evidenced by his new position as a salaried officer of the Steelworkers. A little later, after Murray left the conference room to attend a meeting with Roosevelt at the White House, the executive board voted seventeen to one to declare the office of vice president of the UMW vacant. Thus ended a relationship of more than twenty years between Murray and Lewis as allies and leaders in the American labor movement, first with the UMW and later with the CIO (Dubofsky and Van Tine 1977, 411–12).

The two men remained estranged even up to the death of Murray in 1952. When William Green died that same year, Lewis felt a real loss and had the next UMW convention magnanimously list the AFL president as among the union's "Departed Brothers." Lewis proved unable to make a similar gesture for Murray, whom he could not forgive for his "betrayal" (Proceedings 1956, 290).

Although they had had a close and cooperative relationship for more than two decades, Murray and Lewis were men of vastly different philosophies and temperaments. Lewis was an opportunist; Murray a loyalist. Lewis enjoyed the company of people of wealth and power; Murray preferred to be among more ordinary folk. Lewis cajoled, bullied, and dictated; Murray persuaded, jollied, and persevered. Lewis lacked firm religious beliefs; Murray practiced a form of social democratic Catholicism. Lewis envisioned the labor movement as a force able to exert its will independently, beholden to no one. Thus he could take what Roosevelt gave yet still condemn the president for not giving enough. Murray saw in Roosevelt a president who applied Christian social principles to political practice, was dedicated to the betterment of the working person through trade unionism, and had created the rudiments of a social democratic welfare state. No wonder, then, that the labor movement's "odd couple" eventually experienced such a bitter and irreparable estrangement.

CONSOLIDATING INDUSTRIAL CITIZENSHIP: THE USWA AT WAR AND PEACE, 1939–46

Mark McColloch

We are just leaving a period in which collective bargaining was scarcely ever really accepted. . . . If we go back to such conditions now in view of the present world-wide attacks upon democracy, the outcome may well be a weakening of democratic processes here and a possible setting of the scene for a dictatorship. If American political democracy is to survive, we must succeed. We must have industrial democracy. (Cooke and Murray 1940, 265)

So spoke Philip Murray on the eve of the entry of the United States into World War II. His thought was a powerful and prescient one, but only partially correct. Industrial democracy was not achieved in the steel industry during the war, although large and significant steps were taken to counter industrial tyranny and unchecked corporate domination. More accurately, the record of SWOC and USWA from 1939 to 1946 reflects a balance of gains and failures in the process toward what I will call industrial citizenship. Understanding this process, as Murray wisely noted, also offers important insights into the degree of democratization of broader American life and society in this period.

What follows is not an attempt to write a history of the union from 1939 to 1946. That task requires more work, as do, amazingly, the histories of all the periods of the USWA. Rather, this is an attempt to highlight some of the major transformations wrought and felt by the union, particularly as they shed light upon the theme of industrial citizenship, and to suggest some important areas of study for the future.

The Completion of Organization

The basic prerequisite for industrial citizenship in steel was the establishment of collective bargaining throughout the industry. The completion of this task by SWOC/USWA during World War II probably represented the union's greatest success, one that too generally is taken for granted. It is important to remember just how weakly organized steel was on the eve of the war. Of the major producers, only U.S. Steel and Jones & Laughlin signed contracts with SWOC during the 1936–37 labor upsurge. The other major steel firms—Bethlehem, Republic, Youngstown Sheet and Tube, Inland, Weirton, and Armco—remained aggressively nonunion. Few of the important specialty steel or steel-fabricating firms were unionized. As late as the fall of 1940, Murray could, in confidence, tell the CIO Executive Board that the union had only 250,000 steady dues payers among its approximately one million blue-collar workers (Draham, Dougherty, and Marcus).

The most important of the union's wartime organizing victories came in Little Steel. By August 1942, all four of the firms involved in the bloody strike of 1937—Bethlehem, Republic, Inland, and Youngstown Sheet and Tube—had signed contracts. How did this transformation occur? The marked reduction in unemployment from 1940 to 1942 combined with a more responsive National Labor Relations Board and a vigorous, renewed organizing effort by the union were probably essential in producing this change. For the most part, however, the Little Steel locals and their members disappear from the historiography of the period from the loss of the strike in 1937 to the Little Steel negotiations of 1942.

We do know that the situation in Little Steel was not homogeneous. Throughout the period from 1937 to 1942, SWOC was weakest in the Republic, Weirton, and Armco plants. The 1937 Memorial Day massacre took place at a Republic plant, as did the company-inspired reigns of terror in 1937 in Massillon and Youngstown, Ohio (Galenson 1960, 97–107). The situation was a little better at Inland and Youngstown Sheet and Tube. At Bethlehem, the giant of Little Steel, the scene was complicated by an effective carrot in the form of a credible company union, in existence since 1918, and the stick of repression, most notably in Johnstown and Bethlehem, Pennsylvania (page 107).

Detailed comparative studies of these towns and their unions are needed to determine at what level, if any, SWOC functioned in that five-year period. SWOC rebuilt with surprising effectiveness and speed a few years later, suggesting that the nucleus of the union was maintained in most areas. Golden and Ruttenberg provide a stimulating insight (1942, 113–14) in their claim that the reorganization of Little Steel was possible because the strong and stable ethnic, family, and community networks in the steel towns sustained the badly defeated union cadre during its dark age. We must temper our enthusiasm over this insight, however, by noting that the same authors summarized the organizing appeal of SWOC in 1940 as "join a modern union that can establish collective bargaining peacefully" (page 112), an approach that could have had only limited persuasive value in the Little Steel towns after the repression of 1937.

We do know that SWOC restructured its Little Steel organizing effort in 1940 to take advantage of improved opportunities. The union dissolved several of the old Amalgamated-SWOC lodges, dating from 1933, and replaced them with broader but less autonomous organizing committees (Harbison 1942, 531). Bethlehem, in particular, was targeted. Van Bittner was placed in charge of the drive, and a special edition of *Steel Labor* was published on a regular basis (Galenson 1960, 116). Local studies, Bittner's papers, and the left-wing press could well provide scholars with outlines of these crucial drives.

An important boost in the organizing of Little Steel came in April 1940 when the U.S. Supreme Court refused to review a lower-court decision that Republic's actions in the strike three long years before had been illegal. As a result, Republic had to reinstate seven thousand fired union activists, at a cost to Republic of $2 million (Galenson 1960, 109).

Heartening as this deferred justice was, it was not sufficient to bring Tom Girdler, the chief executive officer of Republic, and his ilk to the bargaining table. A massive and barely studied strike wave at Bethlehem was needed to do that. The battle erupted first in Lackawanna, New York, in February 1941, where thirteen thousand workers walked off their jobs to protest company disciplinary actions against one thousand union supporters. An all-day battle was fought with police in which the strikers held their own. By the next morning, Bethlehem's chairman, Eugene Grace, had agreed to negotiate with SWOC and to settle outstanding grievances, including revocation of the suspensions (Preis 1964, 107). The decisiveness of this event calls out for historians to research the backdrop to the union's ability to reverse the defeat of 1937.

Within weeks, the upsurge spread to Bethlehem, Pennsylvania, where more than 90 percent of the twenty-one thousand workers walked out, prompted by the firm's attempt to hold company-union elections (Preis 1964, 108). SWOC's response to attempts to break the picket lines was to erect its own massive picket lines. The company agreed to recognize SWOC as the bargaining agent for its own members and agreed to a grievance procedure. Thousands of workers celebrated with a twelve-mile-long procession through the streets of the company-dominated town. A young writer watching the marchers as they reached a bridge that divided the town described the event: "They came across, an army terrible with banners." He noted a sign on a building in a working-class neighborhood. It read "The Italo-American Social Club of Bethlehem, Pa. 224 members. One Scab—Charles ("Rocky") Fischetti. Come Back and Get Your Dollar, You Rat" (Kempton 1986).

By then, the huge Johnstown, Pennsylvania, mill was out, also provoked by attempts to hold company-union elections. The walkout was so total there that only token picket lines had to be maintained. No serious attempts were made to break them. Daniel Shield, who had broken the strike of 1937 as the mayor of Johnstown, was now a private citizen and was himself arrested when he appeared near picket lines. Here too workers celebrated their victory with a ten-mile parade through the streets of the city, which would never again be a company town in the old sense (*Steel Labor,* April 18, 1941).

Only in the wake of these strikes did the Circuit Court of Appeals finally uphold an NLRB order dissolving company unions in Bethlehem firms (Hogan 1971, 3:1182). Bethlehem agreed to representation elections at its plants. At Lackawanna, where the union won by a three-to-one margin, SWOC used a car caravan, billboards, union rallies attended by the mayors of Buffalo and Lackawanna, and letters from the local Catholic bishop to generate support (*Steel Labor,* May 23, 1941, and June 25, 1941). Representation elections, strung out from June to October, brought union victories won by margins ranging from four to one at Johnstown to two to one at Bethlehem and Sparrow's Point, Maryland, and three to two at Steelton, Pennsylvania (United Steelworkers cases, 5). The other Little Steel firms— Inland, Youngstown Sheet and Tube, and Republic—soon fell in line. Probably the most interesting of these firms was Republic. The situation following the reinstatement of the fired activists must have been marked by great union activity, for by the time Republic agreed to an NLRB membership check, which was held in August 1941, a substantial majority of its production workers belonged to SWOC. Card counts showed membership ranging from 60 percent at South Chicago and Massilon to 80 percent at Cleveland and Warren (page 7). Again, comparative local studies could tell us much, particularly if they address the intersection of local politics and civil liberties.

A less dramatic but equally significant series of union victories was won at U.S. Steel plants. Although the union had been able to hold on to the contract it had gained in 1937, it was not the exclusive bargaining agent for U.S. Steel workers. Dues picket lines, mobilizing union activists from an entire region, had to be used periodically to reinforce membership. The huge Homestead, Pennsylvania, plant was down to three hundred dues payers by the spring of 1940, and the International was forced to pay the office rent and secretary's salary (Keck 1950, 49).

Comparative studies are needed to trace the patterns of survival and rebirth at U.S. Steel plants in the period from 1937 to 1942, when exclusive bargaining rights were won by a fourteen-to-one vote (*Steel Labor,* June 30, 1942). Though the signing of an improved contract with U.S. Steel in April 1941 is often cited as the crucial milestone (Galenson 1960, 117), the turning point came earlier, at least at some locations. At Homestead, for example, the projected closing of the maintenance department and the layoff of 161 workers, along with a militant response organized through the District 15 office of SWOC, turned around the situation. After more than $10,000 worth of dues were collected in one day from the aroused Homestead workers, the company backed down (Keck 1950, 49–50). Further study may well show a similar pattern at other plants and indicate that the 1941 contract was made possible by a resurgence in the size and militancy of the union, rather than vice versa.

Another target for scholarly research is the successful organization of "small steel," as well as those few sectors that remained nonunion. Dozens of firms, large and small, were unionized by SWOC during 1941 and 1942. During 1942 alone, NLRB elections were won at such traditionally anti-union bastions as Timken Roller Bearing in Canton, Ohio, with more than eleven thousand workers; Baldwin Locomotive in eastern Pennsylvania, with sixty-five hundred; Wheeling (West Virginia) Steel, with twelve thousand; the Pressed Steel Car in McKees Rocks, Pennsylvania, site of the 1909 IWW strike; the Colorado Fuel and Iron Company; and Crucible Steel, with its more than sixteen thousand workers (*Steel Labor,* November 17, 1942). Each of these plants deserves its own chronicler to understand why workers turned to unions in the early 1940s when previous efforts had failed. The Crucible election, in which the union won by a twenty-five-to-one margin at its ten plants after the company had repudiated its 1937 contract, might be the focus of one such study or the election at the Colorado Fuel and Iron plant at Pueblo, where the union had suffered severe defeat only a year earlier. (For more on the Crucible election, see Galenson 1960, 115, and *Steel Labor,* October 23, 1942; for more on Pueblo, see *Steel Labor,* June 25, 1941, and November 17, 1942.)

Clues might come from an examination of the various editions of *Steel Labor*—national, California, Canada, Weirton, New England, and southern—published in 1942. *Steel Labor* also lists targets remaining for organization in 1942. Late wartime growth in Canada and California was substantial, but organizing in the South, which deserves a detailed study of its own, remained weak except in Big Steel plants. In fact, as late as 1944, a majority of the union's members resided in just Pennsylvania, Ohio, and Illinois.

The unionization of the can industry, almost totally organized by 1945, is poorly chronicled. The successful organization of the

iron range, scene of so many earlier heroic but largely unsuccessful organizing efforts, merits a story of its own. By early
1943, it was 75 percent unionized, and the task was completed
by the end of the year (*Steel Labor,* January 22, 1943, and May
28, 1943).

By 1945, the only basic steel companies that were not organized
were Armco and Weirton (USWA Proceedings, 41–42). Detailed
studies of these isolated failures are timely, especially because
what was not accomplished by the USWA during the war never
was. Many workers at both firms are still members of nonaffil-
iated unions which grew out of the old company unions. Clearly,
the repression used by these firms and their dominance in the
small, one-industry towns were critical reasons for the defeats
of the USWA. Weirton Steel, for example, fired nearly one
hundred USWA supporters during 1943 and 1944 (page 58).
Weirton also attacked and beat USWA organizers in a February
1944 riot (*Steel Labor,* December 1944). The company was also
willing to match the wage increases won by the USWA to stave
off unionization. In fact, it was Edwin Weir's announcement in
1941 of a ten-cent wage hike that pushed U.S. Steel and the
USWA to sign a contract that increased wages for union members
by ten cents (Livernash 1961, 239).

By 1944, ten thousand white-collar workers belonged to the
union, and at least that number joined in the next two years
(USWA Proceedings, 42). Small as this number was, it deserves
attention for two reasons. On the one hand, the war years were
one of the most successful periods for organizing salaried steelworkers. Why an important minority turned to unionization at
this time and how their unions functioned are significant questions. On the other hand, the large majority of white-collar steelworkers did not join. Why unionizing efforts failed is equally
critical to an understanding of labor relations in the steel industry
in the postwar period.

Bargaining and the Strike

Perhaps the most studied aspect of the history of the USWA
during the war years is the three-headed negotiations that took

place between labor, management, and government. Two movements are of paramount importance in this intricate dance that occurred from the time of the 1941 negotiations between the USWA and U.S. Steel and Jones & Laughlin through the development of the Little Steel Formula and its modest revisions to the great 1946 walkout. Historians universally discuss the increased involvement of the federal government in steel industry negotiations, a pattern that persisted into the postwar period. This observation has tended to obscure a less clearly understood point of paramount importance to an understanding of industrial citizenship: the improved bargaining position of the union, resulting from the much lower rate of unemployment, the substantially higher membership, and the union's enhanced standing in the community.

As early as the 1941 negotiation, one can see the new position of the union emerging. With joblessness rapidly declining and the upsurge in Little Steel under way, SWOC demanded and won a ten-cents-an-hour raise for U.S. Steel and Jones & Laughlin workers, their first raises since 1937 (Livernash 1961, 239; Tilove 1948, 5). Representation elections had not yet been held, however, so the contract was applicable to SWOC members only (Galenson 1960, 117).

Within a few months, SWOC was seeking further improvements for workers in Big Steel companies, as well as a similar contract with the newly organized Little Steel firms. The famous Little Steel Formula, adopted by the National War Labor Board in July 1942, established a new pattern, including a wage hike of five and a half cents, exclusive bargaining rights, maintenance of membership, and a dues checkoff (Galenson 1960, 118).

The history of bargaining for the next three years focuses on the efforts of the union to break the straightjacket of the Little Steel Formula and attempts by corporations and government agencies to hold the lid on. Though the bureaucratic corporate-government alliance was largely successful, important breaches were made. As early as March 1943, for example, the War Labor Board grudgingly approved a raise for thirty thousand USWA members on the iron range that openly exceeded the Little Steel Formula by five and a half cents per hour (*Steel Labor*, March 26, 1943).

As inflation increased, the USWA mounted its most powerful challenge to the Little Steel Formula. In December 1943, the union served notice on hundreds of firms that it was reopening its contracts and demanding a seventeen-cents-an-hour wage increase (*Steel Case*, 119). On Christmas Eve, distressed over the failure of the War Labor Board to agree to a retroactive date for any settlement it might approve, Philip Murray and the union leadership permitted, and to some extent organized, a major strike. By Christmas, more than 150,000 steelworkers were out, making it the largest walkout in which the USWA had ever participated, and the number rose the next day (*Steel Case*, 119; Preis 1964, 201). The strength of the protest forced President Roosevelt to intervene. In a typical Rooseveltian formula, seized upon by Murray, the president promised "full retroactivity within the Little Steel formula." By New Year's Eve, the strike was over. The WLB took the case, appointed a review panel, and strung the case out until December 1944, after Roosevelt's reelection. The steelworkers were granted a wage boost (although it was posed as an adjustment of wage inequalities), improved shift differentials, and more days of vacation (Hogan 1971, 3:1186). Just as important, the union's action and the WLB's response centralized bargaining into a firm national pattern. The WLB order applied to eighty-six companies, and the steel corporations formed a joint Steel Case Research Committee to present their arguments to the WLB (Tilove 1948, 5–8).

The new contract ran until October 15, 1946, and left open the possibility of reopening it if national wage policy was changed. With the collapse of the Axis, such a change did occur. In response, the union demanded, in its loudest voice ever, a substantial wage increase (Livernash 1961, 245). On October 24, 1945, the WLB formally relinquished jurisdiction over wage negotiations in the industry (Hogan 1971, 3:1612).

A complex and frequently recounted round of negotiations began. Failure to achieve a contract led to a strike, which some historians have seen as a charade by the companies and the union, designed to allow the government to grant price hikes sought by the steel firms. But, unlike the UAW, the USWA never coupled its demands for substantial wage hikes with a call for a hold on prices (Livernash 1961, 252). The delay in launching the strike, its generally peaceful nature, its short duration (twenty-five days), and the fact that the steel firms received all, if not more, of the price increase necessary to offset the raises have strengthened the view of the strike as a charade and have obscured some perhaps more fundamental points (Preis 1964, 270–78).

The most basic of these points is the scope and power of the walkout. The strike was authorized by a vote of five to one by more than 500,000 workers, and all of the basic steel and most of the important fabricating firms participated. In fact, it was the largest strike in American history to that point. The strike was peaceful precisely because it was so powerful and complete and the union so favorably positioned economically, politically, and socially that the steel companies were unwilling to attempt to break it. From location to location, in places that recall the bloody repression of earlier strikes, the walkout was solid. The superintendent of the Homestead mill announced at the onset of the strike that there would be no production for the duration, and the borough fathers chimed in by announcing that they would make no effort to break it. More than nine thousand picketers appeared on the first day. When a rumor spread that supervisors were performing some maintenance jobs, the union mobilized a rally of fifteen hundred to prevent it, attended by the Homestead burgess and the state senator. The company buckled under. In Braddock, the city council joined the picket line en masse, and in Clairton the city government authorized $50,000 in aid to needy strikers (see Sweeney 1956, 62 and 277; Keck 1950, 60–64; *Steel Labor,* February 1946).

The USWA won its wage demand. The seventeen-and-a-half-cent settlement was almost exactly what the union had demanded. From the standpoint of the 1960s and the early 1970s, it has been easy for some historians to consider such a strike and negotiations routine. From the rougher terrain of the late 1980s, such a conclusion is not possible. Those who see the 1946 strike primarily as an exercise in class collaboration at the expense of outsiders must satisfactorily explain why the steel companies were not willing to make such a deal in 1892, 1919, 1937, or, for that matter, 1986. The 1946 strike was a ratification and confirmation of the developments from 1939 to 1945, a process that enabled the union, for the first time, to establish industrial citizenship on the bargaining front.

Composition of the USWA

Who waged the battles for industrial citizenship? Who were the steelworkers, ethnically and racially? What skills did they have? How many women steelworkers were there? How did the composition of the work force change over the course of the war? We have surprisingly few answers to these questions.

Employment in steel expanded during the war, although not as much as in most other industries, including auto and electrical manufacturing. Basic steel employed an average of 408,000 workers in 1939. All the growth occurred over the next three years, peaking at 511,000 in 1942, 22 percent higher than the prewar figure (Hogan 1971, 3:1185). By 1944 employment in basic steel had already declined to 457,000.

It would be misleading, however, to assume that only 100,000 or so new workers were employed or reemployed from 1939 to 1945. For two major reasons, military service and quits, the actual number of new hires had to be many times that. In 1943 the union estimated that 186,000 former members were serving in the U.S. military (*Steel Labor,* March 26, 1943). A year later, when enlistment in the armed forces was at its peak, the number had grown to 202,000 (USWA Proceedings, 49). Monthly turnover rates for male and female steelworkers ranged from 2.0 percent to 5.4 percent in basic steel plants surveyed by the government in late 1943 (Erickson 1944, 32). Thus, if we accept the lower figure (to avoid counting twice those men who left for the service), we find that more than 120,000 steelworkers had to have been hired in 1943 to maintain the size of the work force, or at least 500,000 during the 1940–45 period, even allowing for lower turnover in 1940, 1944, and 1945. On the order of 700,000 workers must have been hired or rehired by basic steel plants during this period.

My attention turns first to the influx of women workers. In 1940, only about five thousand women were employed in basic steel, and another fifteen thousand or so were in steel fabrication. Most of the increase in female employment occurred in 1943

(Ruck 1975, 52). By 1944, the peak for female employment in the industry, the figure had risen to more than eighty thousand, about evenly divided between basic and fabricating. Thus, about 8 percent of the production workers in basic steel were female (Erickson 1944, 42).

Women steelworkers were not distributed evenly throughout the steel region. Pittsburgh had a smaller-than-average number, whereas Chicago boasted more than average (Erickson 1944, 4). Nor were women equally represented throughout the range of occupations. Before the war, almost all the women in basic steel were employed to sort or inspect tinplate (page 3). As the war dragged on, their employment boundaries widened. They remained concentrated, however, in the light and less skilled occupations. Women made up significant percentages of the work force in rolling mills and in fabricating and finishing. The fabrication sections of some basic mills were 25 to 50 percent female. Very few women worked in coking operations or around blast furnaces. By late in the war, women were appearing in maintenance departments, particularly as electricians' helpers and as brick handlers (page 7).

By the end of 1943, women were operating machines and even light cranes, but their access to these jobs was often blocked. The traditional job ladder to crane operator, for example, then and now, included a job doing hooking. Attaching items to be lifted to the crane required considerable upper-body strength and was usually done by strong young men. Few women were given the chance to try a job it was assumed they would not be able to perform. A word of caution is necessary concerning statistics on the distribution of female production workers: Jobs employing the most women were plant clerk and laboratory technician, and although these were nonproduction jobs, they were included in calculating the number of women production workers in a department (Erickson 1944, 11).

Female workers seem to have been recruited primarily from the steel towns. The most detailed study to date identifies them as primarily the wives and daughters of steelworkers, but this claim is built on slender evidence. Most were also newcomers to industrial work who were drawn primarily from the service sector and the ranks of housewives (Erickson 1944, 24).

Women's wages were, as we might suspect, substantially lower than those of men. Women in steel, however, seem more frequently to have been granted equal pay for equal work than women in auto or other industries in which they were employed as cheaper substitutes for men (Erickson 1944, 22). Of course, their low seniority, denial to many departments and of the opportunity to climb job ladders, and the fact that most prewar "boys' " jobs now went to women meant that equal pay for equal work did not bring wage equality (Erickson 1944, 22). The 1941 U.S. Steel contract raised the minimum wage for women to seventy-two cents an hour from the previous fifty-six cents, so both men and women had the same floor rate (*Steel Labor*, April 18, 1941), but by late 1943 most women were still earning less than eighty cents per hour. Further study of corporate personnel records is needed to determine the degree to which women were able to narrow the salary gap in the later war years and the persistent sources of that gap.

We know little about the fate of the eighty thousand distaff workers in the immediate postwar period. The Women's Bureau report in 1943 noted flatly that "it seems to be generally agreed that women's employment is a temporary work expedience" (Erickson 1944, 20). The delayed entry of women meant that few had more than two and a half years' seniority by V-J Day, too little to offset the seniority position of most returning veterans (even if impartial seniority procedures were used), which was not the situation in auto, for example. After the war, the percentage of female workers in steel fell rapidly, to well below even prewar levels. In Pennsylvania there was only a 1 percent drop-off, but in Illinois less than half the total number of female workers in 1940 held jobs in steel a decade later (Rowan 1968, 42–48).

During the war, the turnover rates for women steelworkers were approximately equal to those of men, but the major reasons for quitting were different. Military service was the primary reason men quit, whereas women left because of child-care difficulties. Absentee rates in four basic steel mills studied ranged from 65 to 300 percent higher for women than for men; child-care problems and family illness were listed as the major causes of absenteeism. We should remember, however, that even in the mills with the highest rates of absenteeism among women, 94 percent of the female employees were on the job on any given workday (Rowan 1968, 32–33).

Day-care centers provided little aid to mothers in the steel industry because so many were on rotating shifts, and women expressed little interest in them (Rowan 1968, 25). Clearly, the impact on family life of the influx of women workers demands greater attention. Is it safe to assume that, then as now, grandparents were the major care givers?

What was the role of women in the union? Cursory indications are that it was minimal but expanded rapidly during the war. Eighteen women joined seventeen hundred men as delegates to the 1942 USWA founding convention, at a time when the union was perhaps 5 percent female (Proceedings, 307–41). By 1944, the balance had improved a bit. There were sixty-one women delegates to the second USWA conclave, or about 3 percent of the delegates (Proceedings, 264–306). Half came from just five of the union's thirty-nine districts. By that time, 32 women were presidents of locals, and another 446 women held one of the eight top offices in a local (Proceedings, 42–43). Unfortunately, the figures are unavailable for an earlier period. It will also take more study to learn how much low seniority per se diminished women's chances of being elected to office.

Employment for blacks also rose in steel during the war. In 1940 SWOC claimed thirty-five thousand black members, twenty thousand of whom were in basic steel. By late 1943 the larger union had seventy thousand blacks, half of whom were in basic steel (Proceedings, 43). The number of black employees grew most significantly in the late war years, and by late 1944 the industry's work force was 14 percent Afro-American (Dickerson 1978, 134). There were substantial variations locally. In 1944 blacks constituted 16 percent of the work force in Homestead yet only 4 percent at Bethlehem Johnstown (page 135). Perhaps as important as the gain in employment during the war, employment rates for blacks, unlike those for women, increased into the early postwar period. From 1940 to 1950 the percentage of black steelworkers in Pennsylvania rose from 3.6 to 6.0, in Illinois from 3.7 to 16.2, and in Maryland from 16.3 to 27.5. It fell only in Alabama and not significantly, from 37.7 to 36.5 percent (Rowan 1968, 36).

Black steelworkers were recruited from a variety of sources. In 1940, within the city limits of Pittsburgh alone, 37 percent of the 2,643 black steelworkers were unemployed, double the figure for whites, although most of these workers were hired early in the war. By 1943, recruiters were ranging into the Deep South, particularly Georgia and the Carolinas, for jobs in Pittsburgh and to Mississippi for jobs in Chicago (Dickerson 1978, 96). Already existing migration chains were augmented by the easing of employment barriers for jobs with a living wage.

Wage and occupational discrimination against blacks was most evident in their job segregation. Although the number of departments open to blacks grew during the war and some middle-level jobs were opened for the first time, many sections of the mill, including most of the fast tracks to skilled positions, remained closed (Ruck 1975, 85; USWA Proceedings, First Constitutional Convention, 138). The resulting segregation meant that blacks with greater seniority could be laid off before whites and that newly hired whites could begin at wages higher than those of blacks with four to seven years' seniority.

By the end of the war, blacks had made modest permanent occupational gains. The percentage of blacks who were semiskilled was almost as high as the percentage among whites, 41 percent versus 46.5 percent. Only 16.7 percent of blacks were skilled, however, versus 42 percent of whites. In other words, the overwhelming majority of black steelworkers were unskilled or semiskilled, whereas the overwhelming majority of whites were skilled or semiskilled (Dickerson 1978, 142; Rowan 1968, 31).

The wartime housing situation provides some hints of the additional difficulties black workers faced on and off the job. Blacks were heavily affected by the housing shortage and paid higher rents per square foot. Black neighborhoods were bulldozed in the wartime expansion of the Duquesne and Homestead mills in Pennsylvania. Many dislocated families gained admittance to newly built housing projects, but housing in the Pittsburgh area, among others, remained clearly segregated. Some black steelworkers spent the war living in tiny trailers, if they were lucky, or in bachelors-only quonset hut barracks erected by the federal government. Space was at an even greater premium for blacks in Chicago, and housing segregation there was even more rigid (Dickerson 1978, 140).

Blacks played a growing and important role in the union. I could not determine the percentage of black delegates to SWOC and USWA conventions or the number of black officers of local unions. We do know that more than twenty locals submitted resolutions to the 1942 convention condemning discrimination in the mills and Jim Crow laws in the South and that the resolutions were adopted by the union (Proceedings, 136). That same convention, however, provided black delegates with a list of "colored hotels" in Cleveland, as Secretary-Treasurer David McDonald said, "for the information and guidance of our brothers who do want to go to colored hotels" (page 136). By 1944, such a public statement would not have been made by a top officer of the USWA.

Although the union's executive board remained all white (and all male), the union employed more than twenty blacks on its staff. In response to pressure from Afro-American steelworkers, one black employee, Boyd Wilson, was appointed International representative and charged with monitoring discrimination cases taken up by branches of the union and, when cases were prosecuted, of bringing them to the attention of the various district directors. This task met with mixed results (Augustine 1948, 36).

The attitudes and roles of white officers of locals were very important in determining the extent to which blacks participated in the union. In February 1944, for example, six hundred blacks at Clairton, Pennsylvania, struck over discrimination in upgrading. With the support of the USWA and the Fair Employment Practices Commission, they won an agreement that mandated that future promotions would be awarded equally. Many locals contributed funds to area branches of the National Association for the Advancement of Colored People and participated in employment and upgrading efforts. At a Pullman plant in Chicago, for example, one thousand whites joined an equal number of blacks in a strike over discrimination (Ruck 1975, 78). Hate strikes, such as the one at Colorado Fuel and Iron at Minnequa in May 1944, protesting the employment of blacks in previously all-white departments of the mill, also occurred (page 53).

Blacks strongly backed the 1946 strike. Homestead, for example, had "Negro Days" on the picket line. In general, the situation was the reverse of that in 1919 (Dickerson 1978, 166–67; Draham, Dougherty, and Marcus). We await a study similar to the one by August Meier and Elliot Rudwick on the involvement of black rights activists in the USWA in Chicago to tell us more, although Dennis Dickerson has made a major step forward with his book on Pittsburgh (1986).

Neither women nor blacks account for the majority of workers hired by the steel mills during the war. From whence came these additional forces? Steelworkers who were unemployed in the late 1930s were one vast reservoir. As late as 1940, Pittsburgh alone had six thousand steelworkers who were officially jobless (Dickerson 1978, 96), and retired workers were brought back into the mills. Teen-agers were too as the high school drop-out rate rose markedly during the war years. Other sources of labor were job jumpers, rural white migrants, and Mexicans, particularly in Chicago. More extensive study of personnel files and other documents is needed to determine who the new workers were and how their ethnic and socioeconomic composition influenced their behavior. In fact, ethnicity in general is a historical lacuna during this period. Did the war years accelerate the incorporation of Eastern and Southern European immigrants, or did it only continue at the pace of previous decades?

We do know a little about the job tenure and family size of steelworkers. For instance, in the midst of the flood of new migrants to the industry, some workers were paragons of stability. In basic steel, 59 percent of the workers employed on January 1, 1942, were still there three years later (*Steel Case*, 352). In December 1943, 10 percent of the workers had less than a year of seniority, while another 16 percent had one to two years. A substantial majority of the work force had less than ten years' experience, whereas only one-third had more than fifteen (page 106). At some locations, there was more stability. A typical steelworker in Braddock, Pennsylvania, carried seventeen years' seniority in 1945 (*Steel Labor*, August 1945, 4).

Studies of the tax forms of the 150,000 production workers

employed by U.S. Steel in March 1944 show that the average steelworker's family was composed of the wage earner and two others. One-sixth of the steelworkers listed themselves as single, and about one-third had three or more dependents (*Steel Labor,* August 1945, 4). We must add a note of caution here: employees in general often understate the number of dependents they have to ensure receiving a tax refund the next April. Another study found that steelworkers' families were substantially larger than average. On Pittsburgh's Southside, fully 43 percent of the steel-workers' families had five or more members, and 41 percent did in the neighborhood of Hazelwood. This was in contrast to 32 percent of the families in Pittsburgh as a whole. In Braddock, the average steelworker was married with one child (*Steel Labor,* August 1945, 4). More research on family size and composition, as well as changes brought on by the war, is needed if we are to gain the understanding necessary to produce the sadly needed 1940s version of *The Households of a Mill-town.*

Standard of Living

Scarcely any aspect of the work life of the steelworkers during World War II has been more extensively studied than their wages. This was the case at the time, when wage rates became a major topic of debate at the War Labor Board between the companies and the union. Historians have also debated the question, particularly to generate evidence on the wisdom of the no-strike policy and reliance on the rulings of the WLB.

The broadest outline of the wage picture is clear: gross pay for the average worker outstripped inflation, but hourly straight-time rates did not. Average gross hourly earnings rose by about 40 percent from 1940 to 1945 (Livernash 1961, 137), considerably less than in the auto industry. After factoring in inflation and long hours, one careful observer calculated that real annual earnings for the average steelworker increased by 26 percent during the same period (Lichtenstein 1982, 111). Even accounting for the next several pages of caveats, exceptions, and other limitations, the average steelworker was still grossing substantially more money toward the end of the war than before it.

The standard of living for steelworkers was very low on the

eve of the war. Few received any raises at all from the middle of 1937 until the spring of 1941, when the union won general raises of ten cents an hour, which, at best, equaled the inflation rate of the previous fifteen months (*Steel Labor,* April 18, 1941).

In other words, most steelworkers were earning Depression-level real hourly wages on the eve of Pearl Harbor. This is the base from which wartime gains must be measured. In 1941, the average worker at U.S. Steel grossed $35.92 per week. Those at Bethlehem earned $1.72 more (USWA brief, 258). By January 1942, average earnings had climbed to $39.24 in basic steel, versus $49.36 in auto and a startling $40.47 in electrical manufacturing, which had a heavily female constituency (page 260). According to the Heller budget, established by the famous liberal economist, in February 1942 a family needed an annual income of $2409 to sustain itself at the following level: each adult could have one new coat every six years and a new pair of shoes every two; Dad could afford one and a half dress shirts and a workshirt each year and Mom could afford two housedresses. They and their two or three children lived in a rented apartment of five or six rooms, and they drove an aged used car (pages 297–98).

A few moments with paper and pencil will show that the typical steelworker earned less than 80 percent of what he needed. Unless the family was smaller or there was an additional source of income, even the Heller budget was out of reach. No wonder that, as late as 1943, 15 percent of the nation's steelworkers lived in homes without running water and 30 percent had no indoor bathroom (USWA Proceedings, Second Constitutional Convention, 62).

In February 1944, when steelworkers' earnings were at their high, *Fortune* magazine featured a portrait of a typical steelworker, Dmitr Stoyanoff, who was forty-eight years old and had a wife and three children. He earned $2109 in 1943 on his job at Timken Roller Bearing in Canton, Ohio. He spent more than 40 percent of his gross earnings on food alone. Another $309 went for rent. He drove a 1938 Graham Paige, described by the journalist as having "no cash value," and was unable to purchase war bonds or adult clothing that year. The bulk of the rest of his income was used to pay doctors' bills, buy gasoline to drive to and from work, and repair his family's aging refrigerator. No wonder that *Fortune* noted: "Along Grant Street in Duquesne, in the gray alleys of Homestead and in the company town of Gary, Indiana, men who remember the long agony of the 1930s wonder just when the gravy is going to be dished out to them" (page 216).

During 1940 and 1941, many steelworkers benefited from an increase in their average weekly take-home pay, for the most part because they were working more hours per week. We should not, however, exaggerate the number of people who actually worked forty or more hours each week. Thousands of unemployed or partially employed steelworkers went on a forty-hour-a-week schedule during 1940 and 1941, substantially boosting their gross earnings, yet, for 1941 as a whole, workers averaged only 38.6 hours per week; the figure rose to 39.9 only by late 1942 (USWA brief, 57; *Steel Case,* 224). Part-time work, which was still quite common, particularly in tube mills, accounts for why the average hours worked was less than forty. In early 1942, thirty-four hundred Youngstown Sheet and Tube employees were still working only three to four days a week, as were thirty-two hundred in rolling and finishing at Bethlehem Johnstown. Very few finishing mills operated full time before mid-1942, and even in heavier basic mills, the changeover to war products sometimes brought weeks or even months of layoff (see USWA brief, 57–58 and 248).

The major change in hours and the resulting gain in gross wages did not occur until May 1, 1943, when, in a huge victory for the union, the War Manpower Commission (WMC) established the forty-eight-hour week as the standard in basic steel. The additional eight hours were to be paid at time and a half. For a steelworker going from a forty- to a forty-eight-hour schedule, the potential increase in gross pay was a whopping 30 percent (*Steel Labor,* May 28, 1943).

Hours worked did increase as a result of the order. By January 1944, basic steelworkers were averaging 45.6 hours, the high for the war (Hogan 1971, 3:1185). Clearly, the WMC decision was the equal of the much-touted WLB rulings, such as the Little Steel Formula, in its impact on the standard of living of steelworkers.

Earnings in the two years that followed were the best that the war would bring. Once again, however, several caveats are necessary. The typical steelworker, whether because of absenteeism or plant shutdowns, never averaged a full forty-eight-hour week, and of course the WMC ruling did nothing about hourly wage rates. One company official testified, in a frank statement that speaks volumes about corporate attitudes: "If the most illiterate and unskilled employee of one of these companies, direct from the cotton field, where he earned at best $1 a day, will work the 40 hours per week which the government requires the steel companies to work, he will earn more then $1600 a year" (*Steel Case*, 930). In other words, steelworkers at the bottom of the pay scale still earned incomes well below what they needed to sustain the bare-bones Heller budget, even if they worked a forty-eight-hour week.

Nonetheless, by late in the war the average steelworker was working a longer work week and as a result had increased his gross earnings so that he was ahead of the consumer price index. Several considerations besides the longer work week came into play, however, in evaluating the real value of his take-home pay. One is whether price increases in the crowded steel towns and neighborhoods were higher than the national average. In a two-year period beginning in October 1939, most white steelworkers in the Canton-Massilon area incurred at least a 20 percent increase in rent, and two-thirds of their black counterparts experienced even greater hikes. Food prices in Gary increased by 42 percent in just one year (USWA brief, 89–91). One CIO study of fifteen hundred steelworkers found that their actual cost of living rose twice as fast as the official national rate for 1941–42 (Preis 1964, 214). Increased taxation also took a larger share of gross earnings. In 1940, the family of the average steelworker paid just $16 in federal income tax. By 1943, the figure was $166 for a family of four (*Steel Case*, 382).

By late in the war, a typical Braddock steelworker was earning $50.85 per week. Family income, on average, was less than $6 higher and came from boarders or the earnings of other family members. A majority of the workers there said that they were postponing necessary medical care for financial reasons. Even so, 45 percent of them finished the year having spent more than they had earned (*Steel Labor*, April 28, 1944, 7, and August 1945, 4).

The earnings of steelworkers varied enormously depending

on their skills, the city in which they lived, and even the corporation for which they worked. As might be expected, wages were substantially lower in the South. In 1942, the starting rate for common labor in the South was 60.5 cents versus 72.5 cents in the North (*Steel Case,* 930). Actual average earnings varied even more. Basic steelworkers in Birmingham made 60.3 cents an hour in mid-1943, versus 78.2 cents in Pittsburgh and 79.1 cents in Chicago. Even workers in Baltimore and Youngstown averaged 78 cents. In other words, the average Chicago steelworker outearned his or her southern cousin by more than 31 percent (*Steel Case,* 969–71). The union was only partially successful in narrowing this differential during the war. As late as 1946, wages at Tennessee Coal and Iron lagged 17.5 cents behind the average for workers in other subdivisions of U.S. Steel (Stieber 1959, 250).

Differentials based on skill were even wider. In 1938, the average hourly earnings of workers classified as skilled ranged from 140 to 268 percent that of the unskilled, depending on the company (Stieber 1959, 237). Variations across occupations were often even greater. In 1941, common laborers in basic steel earned 72.5 cents per hour, while rollers in one firm were making $4.05 (Golden and Ruttenberg 1942, 304). Many examples of 400 percent differentials could be found.

One of the union's greatest accomplishments in this period was to narrow this internal gap, which was so large as to be divisive. This was a conscious decision by the union. The three wage increases of 1941, 1942, and 1946 were all on a cents-per-hour basis, narrowing the percentage gap. By 1946, a total of thirty-four cents per hour had been added to the paychecks of all steelworkers. This sum amounted to more than 50 percent of the prewar rate for common labor but less than 20 percent that of a skilled worker making two dollars an hour prewar (Stieber 1959, 239). During the battle for the postwar wage increase Philip Murray argued that workers at all skill levels should receive equal cash raises so as to "achieve a more equitable distribution of the increase among workers" (Hogan 1971, 3:1162). Finally, monetary gains won by the union in the 1944–45 WLB settlement were used to compress wage inequalities.

How much of an increase in wages the average steelworker

gained during the war depended very much on who he or she was. One reason is that the high turnover and expansion of operations, backed by the improved seniority systems, gave steel-workers who remained on their jobs higher-than-average mobility up the job ladder. The earnings of persisters—those employed both before and during the war—grew more rapidly than those of the group as a whole. (The average included hundreds of thousands of new workers, who usually started at wages somewhat below those whose jobs they filled.) From 1941 to 1944 the 60 percent or so of the workers who were persisters saw their weekly earnings rise by 62.4 percent, to $58.50 per week, or about 11 percent more than the average (*Steel Case*, 353).

By late in the war, steelworkers were enjoying their highest real earnings ever. Even though their salaries reflected considerable overtime, their standard of living had improved. When overtime and earnings were curtailed after V-E Day, the resulting shock (the average steelworker lost fifty-two dollars a month because of the reduction in hours) clearly influenced the intensity and unanimity with which steelworkers stood on picket lines in 1946 calling for substantial wage increases (Dickerson 1978, 197). What steelworkers fought for, and won, albeit in a garbled way, was forty for forty-eight.

Despite all the resistance to higher wages that corporations expressed during the war, wage costs, which were only about 35 percent of total costs at the beginning of the war, fell to three-quarters of their prewar level over the course of the conflict (Livernash 1961, 159; USWA brief, 92).

What remains now is to provide some details about the hours worked during the war. As early as 1941, SWOC won an important concession from U.S. Steel. Within the framework of a forty-hour week, most steelworkers had a forty-eight-hour stretch in which no work was scheduled. In other words, for the first time, about 85 percent of the steelworkers could enjoy a weekend, even if it fell on Wednesday and Thursday, and they received premium pay for Saturday and Sunday work (*Steel Labor*, April 18, 1941). Thus tens of thousands of steelworkers could assume a more normal lifestyle. Under the pressure of the early war, however, the union, as did almost all of its CIO counterparts, abandoned overtime pay for Saturday and Sunday per se. Critics of this move should realize that it would have been difficult for the union to campaign for a mandatory forty-eight-hour work week, with time and a half for anything over forty hours, while retaining the additional premium. Nevertheless, the decision provoked a storm of protest at the union's founding convention (Proceedings, 80–90).

Before we envision steelworkers spending at least a day at home each week with their children, even if it was a school day, we must take into account shift work. Fully 64 percent of steelworkers rotated shifts, and only 28 percent worked steady daylight (*Steel Case*, 706). Social and cultural historians could provide much-needed information on the impact such schedules had on family and community life, as well as on the union.

The union did succeed in ending one major hours abuse. By filing a suit, which was upheld by the courts under the Fair Labor Standards Act, for portal-to-portal pay on the iron range, the USWA compelled ore operators to reduce unpaid travel time by one-third to one-half for the duration of the war by increasing the number of gates and improving planning (Proceedings, First Constitutional Convention, 76). Of course, the bitter and successful strike struggles waged by the United Mine Workers over the same issue may have pushed the companies a long way in the right direction.

Today, the two big-ticket items in fringe benefits are pensions and health insurance. To understand the standard of living of steelworkers in the early 1940s, we must immediately note that neither existed, at least not in the form of generally available, company-provided benefits. No wonder so many "retired" steelworkers returned to jobs during the war once they became available. Historians will have to examine the lifestyles and retirement decisions of aged workers. They will also have to probe the methods by which steelworkers cared for their own and their family's health. (Neglect was undoubtedly common, and neighborhood physicians not only made house calls but charged modest amounts and were willing to accept credit.)

The union won some gains in paid vacations during the war. By 1942, an employee could take a week's vacation after three years of work. The old contract had allowed such vacations only after five years. Workers who had more than fifteen years' seniority—one-third of the work force—were given two weeks of vacation (*Steel Case,* 706). The 1945 WLB order won by the union allowed for a week's vacation after one year on the job and for two weeks after five years (Hogan 1971, 3:1186).

Spartan as these rest periods were, in 1943 fully 78 percent of all steelworkers eligible for vacations elected to work that week and collect double pay. Only 22 percent had exercised a similar option in 1941 (*Steel Case,* 1024). Pressure, patriotism, inflation, and a desire to make hay while the forty-eight-hour sun shone motivated their decisions. Five holidays, which paid at double time (at least half of all steelworkers had to work on Christmas, Thanksgiving, and other major holidays), completed the fringe benefit package; three holidays were added in 1945 (Sweeney 1956, 212).

The Shop Floor

To what extent did the consolidation of industrial citizenship extend inside the plants? To answer this question even tentatively, historians must enter a forbidding labyrinth of numbers and local practices and confront such minotaurs as incentive takeout, wage inequalities, seniority units, and five-step grievance procedures. There is no other way out. Let us arm Clio with a stop watch, a clipboard, and a chariot crammed with local contracts and begin our journey.

At the beginning of the war, about half the steelworkers were on an incentive plan (Harbison 1942, 55) and thus their hourly base rate (most had a very low hourly minimum) was of less importance to their wage than the tightness of their incentive rates. A vast complex of factors determined whether an incentive worker "made out," that is, surpassed the 100 percent goal necessary to receive premium payments, and how high the payout would climb.

The percentage of workers on incentive clearly grew during the war, with the union's uneasy blessing. The union agreed to reverse its earlier policy of mild opposition to further incentive plans for two reasons: to boost production as part of the war effort and to secure increased wages for workers, which the WLB not only sanctioned but encouraged. At an Inland Steel barrel factory in Chicago, the company instituted incentive plans for some workers to boost production. Rates were initially loose to smooth acceptance, and workers easily received 120 to 130 percent of their former wages. Soon, all workers in the plant were demanding to be placed on incentive, and a major battle over the tightening of rates was fought for the duration of the war (Whyte 1951, 20–27). SWOC/USWA continued to oppose grossly unfair plans, such as the infamous Bedaux. In its 1941 and 1942 contracts it gained the right to grieve unfair new rates (*Steel Labor*, April 18, 1941).

By the end of the war, fully 65 percent of all steelworkers were on piecework, but there were tremendous local variations in this figure. Studies of four basic steel plants showed that in 1943, 45 to 79 percent of their workers were on incentive plans, with the greatest variations in coking, blast furnace, and maintenance operations. Pittsburgh plants had a higher percentage on incentive than the national average (Stieber 1959, 218).

The average incentive worker outearned his straight-time counterpart, and this gap, which the companies would strive to reduce over the next fifteen years, expanded during the war (Livernash 1961, 218). The highest incentive earnings were in open-hearth, hot-strip, and bar mills and, to a lesser extent, in blooming and slabbing (Stieber 1959, 254). The higher earnings came, however, at a price. U.S. Steel described in its job classification manual the effort it considered to be "a fair day's work": the effort required for a man walking on level ground at three miles an hour. Extended over a forty-eight-hour week, this is tougher than it sounds. The piecework pace was designed to be faster than that (page 176). Labor historians will need to probe deeper into the incentive systems used, the degree of difficulty required for workers to make out, the shop floor battles over new rates, and their impact on workers' health, consciousness, and solidarity.

To an outsider, the first words that come to mind at the mention of a union contract are often wages and seniority. During the war, however, seniority in steel was largely left to individual locals and plant management to negotiate (Ruck 1975, 77). The untutored observer may also imagine that unionization brought something like plantwide seniority, another dolefully untrue assumption. Each local was free to, or, rather, saddled with, negotiating its own seniority units (Ulman 1962, 79).

There were no standardized boundaries for the units. Instead, divisions, departments, and even sections were subdivided. Some large plants had only a dozen or so seniority units. Others, such as Bethlehem's Lackawanna plant, had eighty-one and U.S. Steel at Homestead had even more. Many plants further complicated the issue by having plantwide units for various occupations (Ruck 1975, 77).

Few seniority units were created *de novo* during the war. For the most part, those firms already under contract with SWOC formalized their units in 1937–38. Once established, they seem to have undergone little change. Even in newly organized firms, old patterns of promotion and layoff largely determined the shape of the units. A dissertation might focus on this issue, balancing as it does custom, equity, race, ethnicity, gender, and internal union politics.

Furthermore, negotiation of a seniority unit did not mean that all promotions, shift changes, job bumping, and layoffs were conducted strictly on the basis of longevity. Even with the 1942 seniority rules in basic steel, "ability" and "physical fitness" were given great weight in upgrading and bumping. Only if those two factors were roughly equal was longevity to be the deciding consideration (*Steel Labor,* September 25, 1942). Because the toughest jobs were usually on the bottom of the ladder and there was not much downward bumping during the war, we can assume that the importance of "physical fitness" can be minimized. But other qualifiers were also used. At the beginning of the war, local residency and family status were given weight in the decisions. With union blessing, these two factors were, however, dropped by the end of the war. Furthermore, after 1942, layoffs and recall rights were determined mainly by length of service (McKinley 1952, 15).

Seniority protections did not apply during a probationary period of one to six months, and layoffs or disability absences of more than two years broke seniority (McKinley 1952, 14 and 18). Most plants had an entry or floor labor pool on which the promotional ladder rested. Units could also agree to work reduced hours down to thirty-two rather than allow junior members to lose their jobs. We do not know how long this tradition continued in steel, or how frequently it was exercised, save that it was dropped from the contract in 1948.

Among the most chaotic and feudal aspects of prewar shop life in steel were the wage rates and job classifications. It is estimated that there were more than fifty thousand job titles or classifications, each with its own wage determination. A comparison of essentially identical jobs in four different plants found a wide range of rates. The same jobs on a coke oven were 10 to 15 cents apart, ore bridge operators in blast furnaces were 26 cents apart, scarfers in slab mills were 38.5 cents apart, and bar mill chargers had a range of 39.5 cents. Tradition, favoritism, and accident all played a role in determining the rate structure, a legacy of the reorganization of the work process at the turn of the century (Stieber 1959, 286).

The classification anarchy caused friction within the union, as well as between workers and management. As many as two-thirds of all SWOC grievances were filed over this issue, and from 1942 to 1945, three-quarters of these grievances involved the wages of just one person (Stieber 1959, 45; Lichtenstein 1982, 273).

The union groped for a way out of this chaos without imperiling worker cohesiveness. Initially, management resisted this effort, but by war's end it had been pushed to a position of agreeing with the USWA. The 1937 U.S. Steel contract had allowed internal plant wage inequities to "be taken up for local plant adjustment and settlement made on a mutually satisfactory basis" (Stieber 1959, 4–5). At a time when the union was weak, this left matters largely in management's hands. The improved 1941 contract spoke to the issue of new rates. In return for agreeing to let U.S. Steel use job evaluation methods to set new rates (they had already been doing so for at least thirty years), the union agreed that grievances on new rates could go to binding arbitration, where they would be reviewed in relation to the existing plant structure and job requirements. The 1942 contracts provided for joint committees to study the inequity question, but after a few conferences, the committees dissolved in failure (Stieber 1959, 5; USWA Proceedings, 47).

In late 1943, twelve steel firms, including all the giants except

Bethlehem, undertook a cooperative wage study in an attempt to systematize and standardize their rates. Some historians, in light of this corporate move, have viewed this wage equalization process backwards. They overlook the reason that the anarchy and inequity had become intolerable for management was because workers, via the union, could and did grieve and strike effectively over the issue (Stieber 1959, 26–27; Stone 1973, 53–54). Furthermore, a 1944 WLB order, which was issued in response to the demands of the USWA, called for the diminution of wage inequities through a joint evaluation committee and ordered a 5.5 cents per hour per worker wage increase to be applied toward the solution of the issue. Only then did the companies begin serious negotiation with the USWA over wage inequities (Hogan 1971, 3:1182).

Detailed studies were soon under way. The USWA agreed to the continued use of job evaluations in determining wages in return for the opportunity to give a large percentage of its members raises and to eliminate a major source of headaches. Benchmark occupations and outlines of the plan were agreed to in October 1945 (Livernash 1961, 247). By 1947, all steel jobs were classified into one of just thirty levels, spaced evenly on the wage scale, and almost all the jobs were arranged on standardized promotion ladders (Stieber 1959, 247).

Katherine Stone, the most perceptive observer of how management reorganized work at the turn of the century, argues that the events of the period from 1944 to 1947 were part of "the process by which steel employers tried to break down the basis for unity amongst steelworkers" (1973, 20). She adds that "the labor system set up by the steel employers early in the century was not changed significantly after 1920" (page 54). I would argue just the opposite. Although the new classification system did not restore workers' control (exercised even in the semimythical past by only a skilled minority of steelworkers), it did eliminate a major system of injustices and strengthen union cohesion. Workers could still fight one another over access to job ladders and companies could still discriminate in hiring into seniority units, but the possibility of two workers doing exactly the same job in the same firm for different amounts based on currying favor with the boss was seriously reduced and the need for costly battles over individual grievances was eliminated. Furthermore, the differentials between most jobs were reduced (Stieber 1959, 286). The red-circling of rates on the high side of the new classifications meant that the reorganization did not come at the expense of rate cuts for some workers. The union had taken a significant step toward industrial citizenship and the rule of shop law and away from the whimsical and arbitrary command system.

The expanded strength of the union in the war years brought changes in grievance procedures both *de jure* and *de facto*. Among these changes, and evidence of workers' progress toward industrial citizenship, was the codification of grievance and arbitration procedures. It is possible to misjudge the significance of this process, for the procedures did not address all the problems of workers. We should therefore compare it not only to the ideal of industrial democracy or a vision of an always-militant group of workers, ready at a moment's notice to take major risks on disputes involving small numbers or minor issues, but with the industrial tyranny in the years before 1937.

There was no real grievance procedure in steel before the union. The basic framework was established in the 1937 U.S. Steel contract, which outlined a five-step procedure, culminating in binding arbitration. This final step could be reached only if both sides agreed to it, and they rarely did (Schratz 1954, 154). The 1941 contract with U.S. Steel represented an important step forward for the union. Specific time limits were fixed for each step in the process. Furthermore, in cases involving firings, an employee had to be given a five-day suspension, during which cooler heads might prevail and the union could organize a defense. The union could also mandate that such cases be submitted to arbitration (*Steel Labor*, April 18, 1941). The 1942 contract went further. Arbitration was made the universal final step (*Steel Labor*, September 25, 1942). The 1945 contract replaced the third-party umpire system with a Board of Conciliation and Arbitration (Schratz 1954, 155).

We know almost nothing about the daily fight over grievances in steel. Detailed studies of such grievances, perhaps initially focused on records pertaining to the precedent-setting fifth step, are badly needed. One thing is certain. It was harder to fire someone at war's end than before, and workers had a more favorable prospect for the resolution of their complaints than at any time in the past. Industrial democracy had not been achieved, but no longer was there unchecked tyranny.

Portraits of a technologically backward, stagnant steel industry are false for the war period, when the low unemployment masked the impact of technology on the workers. Even the late 1930s saw major technological change. Most important was the introduction of continuous automatic strip mills, which displaced as many as eighty-four thousand workers in the 1935–40 period and created ghost towns such as New Castle, where 64 percent of the population was on relief. Other mechanization-based unemployment included the replacement of chippers by scarfing machines, the building of butt-weld pipe mills, and the installation of continuous drawing machines in wire mills (see Proceedings, Second Wage and Policy Convention, 60–61, and Harbison 1942, 567).

The number of blast furnaces in operation in the United States remained about constant during the war, with the vast majority the open-hearth type. Nonetheless, about twenty new furnaces went on line during the war. With an average capacity of 400,000 tons, they replaced furnaces with an average tonnage one-tenth that. Of course, the bigger the furnace, the greater the tonnage that could be produced per worker (Hogan 1971, 3:1136). The life span of furnace linings, which were a labor-generating task to replace, was increased by 50 percent. Some modern plants expanded operations, but as the nickname of the Irvin Works ("The Big Morgue") indicates, they employed far fewer workers than their counterparts ("The Steelworkers," 18).

Total tonnage did rise during the war, but far less than one might imagine, and less than in auto, electrical manufacturing, and other industries. The 1940 output of 67.1 million tons topped the 1937 high and was much higher than in 1938 and 1939. It rose to 82.8 million tons in 1941. It crept up through 1944, when it hit the wartime high of 89.6 million tons, before falling back (Hogan 1971, 3:1185).

New plants were opened, particularly in the West. The government built an integrated mill in Geneva, Utah. Kaiser opened its Fontana, California, works, and Armco built a new operation in Houston. Tonnage west of the Mississippi more than doubled during the war, and operations in the South grew as well (Hogan 1971, 3:1454).

Output per worker increased by about 19 percent during the war (Livernash 1961, 159). But greater tonnage, the expansion of exports, and the total collapse of imports meant that the number of workers was not reduced. Clearly, the new technology also altered the skill mix by requiring fewer unskilled workers but more skilled.

Days after Pearl Harbor, Robert Brown, twenty-six, and Joseph Krotz, thirty, workers at Latrobe Electric Steel, were struck by a hot ingot and died almost immediately. They were typical of scores of their peers. On August 26, 1943, a section of the Ferro Enamel Plant in Cleveland exploded. The resulting death of eight USWA members was the worst of many such wartime accidents to workers in the industry. It is instructive to remember that, until D-Day, more steelworkers perished inside the plants than in the war. Students of the work process in steel need to devote far greater attention to the question of safety. (For details on the plant tragedies, see *Steel Labor,* March 27, 1942, and August 26, 1943).

Union Democracy and Internal Life

The internal life of SWOC and the USWA was consolidated during the war, and steps toward democratization were taken. The establishment of the USWA was a prerequisite for formal democracy within the union. The leadership of SWOC credited the successful completion of the unionization of the industry in 1941 as the key factor in delaying the transition from SWOC to the USWA. To this one can add a desire to establish a power base fully independent of the UMWA and pressure from below. Resolutions and debate at the 1940 SWOC policy convention spurred Murray to promise that there would be a constitutional convention within two years. At the time, the organizational outlook in Little Steel was doubtful and relations with Lewis and the UMWA were still good (see Proceedings, Second Wage and Policy Convention, 106).

The legacy of the UMWA-based leadership persisted through

the war. Of the four officers elected in 1942, only Clinton Golden had not been a long-term officer or employee of the UMWA. As late as 1940, two-thirds of the district directors were UMWA officials who were still on that union's payroll (Livernash 1961, 21), although many steelworkers were replacing miners as union staff members (Proceedings, 68).

Much has been made of the top-down character of the USWA constitution. The legacy of Lewis and the UMWA is clear here. As in most unions, the rules of SWOC clearly stated that "no strike shall be called without the approval of the SWOC" (Ulman 1962, 14). The president appointed all the union's staff, a formidable power. During World War II, Murray usually delegated this power to his former secretary, McDonald (page 132), and by 1942 the union employed 502 persons so chosen (Proceedings, 68).

Perhaps as important, a host of other nonconstitutional provisions gave great power and authority to the International. Fourth- and fifth-step grievance procedures were in their hands (Ulman 1962, 81). The initial dues apportionment within the union was seventy-five cents per month to the International and twenty-five cents per month to the locals (page 35). The organization and rules of the conventions strongly favored and approved policies of the incumbents. About 21 percent of the delegates to the 1944 conclave were staff members. In the five days of that convention only forty of twenty-three hundred delegates got the floor, and Murray's speeches alone took up about half of all convention time (Preis 1964, 278). No roll-call votes were taken at the 1942 or 1944 USWA convention (Ulman 1962, 111). (This would have taken hours, and only a few delegates sought it.) In addition, only about half the locals were represented, considerably fewer than in the 1950s and 1960s (page 113). Amendments and substitute resolutions were not permitted, giving great power to the framers of resolutions (Livernash 1961, 82).

Murray's popularity (public-opinion surveys [Mills 1948, 44] found him among the most well-known and well-liked labor leaders of the day, in and out of the USWA) was another factor in the centralization of power. His election to the presidency was totally unopposed.

Nelson Lichtenstein, the leading historian of the wartime CIO, has characterized Murray as "an insecure man who sought consensus and stability," who "had none of the inner calm of one comfortable with great power," and who "thought it threatened his manhood and felt humiliated when other union leaders contradicted him in public or private" (1982, 45). True as this may be of his dealings with the CIO and with Lewis, this is not the man one sees in the wartime SWOC/USWA. Sometimes indulgent, sometimes stern, and authoritarian, but always in charge, Murray dominated the stage. What opposition he had did not appear to threaten him seriously.

Murray's authority and popularity were well rewarded. The founding USWA convention pegged his salary at $20,000 (Proceedings, 234), the highest in the CIO and $2,000 more than he had received from the Miners (Preis 1964, 171). Additional perks included a new Mercury given to him by the UAW in 1941 (*Steel Labor*, November 28, 1941).

The salaries of district directors and staff members were initially much closer to those of the membership. Directors made $360 per month (raised to $500 in 1944), whereas field representatives received $300 per month and a maximum of $3 per day for expenses (Proceedings, First Constitutional Convention, 44, and *Steel Labor*, May 1944, 11).

In some respects, the steelworkers' union was more democratic than most. After 1942, International officers were elected by referenda. District directors, elected for terms of two years, were chosen the same way (Ulman 1962, 98). The International Executive Board, composed of national officers and district directors, was not a rubber-stamp body. It met twenty-three times from 1942 to 1945 and hammered out important decisions (Ulman 1962, 121–24).

Although Murray's reelections were unchallenged, district director bouts, some of which were lost by administration-backed incumbents, were contested. Internal skirmishing also occurred following Murray's heart attack in 1941. To allay this reaction, *Steel Labor* headlines announced that Murray was fine, although he was just out of intensive care (Ulman 1962, 129–31).

Much less is known about the crucial functioning of the union on the local level. At any given point during the war, the union had at least thirty thousand local officers and stewards (USWA brief, 206). We know little of their changing composition, tenure in office, ideology, or functioning. We do know that the responsibilities of the locals grew. Expenses, particularly arbitration costs, rose (Ulman 1962, 35), forcing many to raise dues to $1.25 or $1.50 by 1944. Local contract supplements had to be negotiated to govern crew size and rest periods, work scheduling, and wash-up time, as well as the incentive and seniority provisions already discussed (page 79). We need a series of detailed comparative studies before we can say much more.

Participation in the union varied. The 1942 contracts provided that there would be one steward per five hundred workers in the huge plants and one per two hundred workers in shops with fewer than five thousand members (*Steel Labor*, September 25, 1942). As always, membership attendance at most meetings was low. At the Pittsburgh Jones & Laughlin local, 1272, with a membership of about forty-five hundred workers, attendance at monthly meetings averaged about sixty during 1944–45. At the meeting at which the strike-authorization vote was taken, held in December 1945, interest swelled to 181, or about 4 percent of the membership (Augustine 1948, 37). Was this the pattern throughout the union? Did attendance grow or diminish over the course of the war, and what are we to make of the phenomenon of low attendance?

In 1944, the CIO's Aluminum Workers of America (AWA) joined the USWA (Ulman 1962, 90). With its turbulent history, the organization deserves its own chronicler. Thereafter, locals and officers of the AWA played a major role in several USWA districts. Its former president, Nick Zonarich, became an important International representative. This merger, which set the pattern for the many future amalgamations into the USWA, accelerated the process by which the union's jurisdiction was broadened.

One of the most studied features of the wartime CIO is the wildcat strike, of which a substantial number occurred in steel. More than thirty-one thousand USWA members struck in 1942, in 352 incidents, and there were 993 walkouts the next year (*Steel Case*, 872). In fact, if one includes the semi-official Christmas-week strike, as many work hours were lost to strikes in 1943 as in 1941. Even more walkouts occurred in 1944 (Preis 1964, 226), and at the Homestead plant, job actions were frequent throughout 1945 (Draham, Dougherty, and Marcus).

Nonetheless, we should not exaggerate the significance of wildcats. An average of only thirty workers were involved in each of the 1942 strikes, and there was never a major strike wave (Lichtenstein 1982, 187). We know little about the issues involved in these strikes or their composition and results other than that "wage matters" seemed to have been at the center of half of them (page 273). There was enormous variation in the number of wildcats from firm to firm and from plant to plant. One local alone, 2635, lost 88,500 worker-hours from 1942 to 1944. Not surprisingly, Republic was a strike center. Major causes of walkouts there were scheduling, wage rates, disciplines, maintenance of membership, the slowness of the WLB to act, and, in one hate strike, the desegregation of a washroom (*Steel Case*, 876–83).

Sometimes the leadership came down hard on the wildcats and in support of the no-strike pledge. When workers at Cleveland's American Steel and Wire walked out in 1943, the International Executive Board suspended all the local officers and the grievance committee and put the local in receivership. The Selective Service joined in and immediately inducted the local president into the Navy (Preis 1964, 226). At the 1944 convention, Murray favored upholding the pledge, warning, "You either accept the reasonable voluntary method of doing business in the United States during the course of the war or you accept regimentation or legislative compulsion of some description" (Proceedings, 135). When warnings were not enough, a special IEB meeting was held to discuss the suppression of the strikes (*Steel Case*, 876).

Yet the union also sheltered militants. The USWA filed grievances over most discipline cases involving the wildcats (*Steel Case*, 876) and even protected the leaders of a number of strikes. Murray admitted (in an unsuccessful attempt to shut off debate on the question at the 1944 convention) that "I know that the foremen and managerial forces in many of our plants throughout the country have taken advantage of our no-strike commitment" (Proceedings, 135). Seven resolutions condemning the pledge were submitted to the convention, but many more upheld it. About one-fourth of the delegates seemed to oppose the pledge in the voice vote on the issue (Preis 1964, 728).

Much has been made of the growing bourgeoisification of union officials during the war. In the case of steel, this interpretation relies heavily on a few quotations from Golden and Ruttenberg. There is the striking description of John Witherspoon and Bud Barton, "now substantial citizens in their communities. Both found it hard to change over from fighting management at every step to co-operating on the basis of equality" (1942, 58). Golden and Ruttenberg follow with a description of the firing of a union critic, an operation arranged by the union. These claims need to be examined closely. Golden and Ruttenberg's book was not intended to be a definitive history but rather to win sympathy for collective bargaining among the literate public and personnel officials. One must remember too that by war's end Ruttenberg was the vice president of a steel corporation and Golden was in Washington, far removed from local-level union affairs (Brooks 1978, 208; Stieber 1959, 350). Detailed local studies, depicting the push and tug of conflicting pressures on union activists, are necessary if we are to gain any real understanding of this issue.

Politics, the State, and the Communities

It is generally agreed that the federal government played a greater role in labor relations during World War II than before. At the macro level, historians have looked at the crucial impact of such agencies as the War Labor Board, the War Production Board, and the NLRB on labor relations. Missing is a detailed look at how unions participated in such organizations and their impact not just on the agencies but their internal life.

Key USWA officials were assigned to government agencies. Murray sat on the National Defense Mediation Board (although he privately opposed its creation) until the labor walkout in 1941 (Lichtenstein 1982, 15). Van Bittner was placed on the WLB, and Murray complained to associates that he leaned too much toward harmony with the public and management members (Brooks 1978, 208).

Steelworkers played particularly important roles on the War Production Board. Clinton Golden was vice chairman, and Ruttenberg was assistant director of its steel division (Proceedings, Second Constitutional Convention, 32). Virtually every district of the WPB had a USWA representative on it. More than four hundred production committees were registered by the union with the agency (Proceedings, 66).

In some crucial respects, Murray's January 1941 proposal to Roosevelt entitled "How To Speed Up Steel Production," was, without acknowledgment, adopted by the government. Murray advocated a tripartite industry council which would organize steel into a single production unit. The plan had as its foundation the creation of a "Top Scheduling Clerk" for the entire steel industry (Golden and Ruttenberg 1948, 325; Harbison 1942, 569). The union continually addressed production bottlenecks, such as the shortage of armor plate for tanks, counterposing their high productivity and full-employment plans to private-profit chaos and inefficiency (*Steel Labor,* July 31, 1942). The centralizing aspects of this process to some extent "took," but the issue of democratic planning and control found little sympathy in the postwar years, despite the union's persistent pleas. Perhaps the clearest and most eloquent of the statements made by the USWA appeared in *Steel Labor* on May 28, 1943. The union called the war a "fight for our life" and urged a "substantial down-payment now on the four freedoms." It called for the democratization of American society, especially the Jim Crow South, and listed a formidable agenda to meet specific social needs. Only central planning, added the union, with an important role played by labor, could ensure such a future.

The citizenship role of the USWA was perhaps weakest in the foreign policy realm. Rarely was the union consulted, let alone heeded, during the gigantic events of 1939–46, particularly in the first half of the conflict. Opposition to American involvement in World War II ran high at the 1940 SWOC convention, a little noted fact. Perhaps that is not surprising in a union in which the UMWA, under Lewis, was still such an influence. Nor in a union whose Canadian members, already at war, had seen the government jail many of its CIO leaders to suppress dissent concerning the conflict.

More than a dozen locals sent in antiwar resolutions (only the thirty-hour week and the proportion of dues to go to the locals drew more) (Proceedings, Second Wage and Policy Convention, 279–414). Murray opened the convention by noting that "our nation is entering a period of hysteria, all attributable to the deadly repercussions of a great, devastating war which is now raging in Europe" (pages 6–7). In calling for a policy of strict neutrality, he noted that "the moral issues involved in the current conflict are overshadowed by considerations of power politics that have dominated the actions of the belligerents for several centuries" (page 71). He left the door open, however, by stating that should the nation go to war, it would receive the union's total support. By the 1942 convention, with the Axis in conflict with the Soviet Union and the United States, there was not a hint of antiwar feeling.

In fact, the 1942 USWA convention received eighteen resolutions calling for the opening of a second front and passed a fairly strong version of one (Proceedings, 78). This may remind us that considerably more research is needed on the role of the left in the union, especially of the Communist party, after 1937. An examination of the growing ties between the State Department, the OSS and its ilk, and the union would be valuable. We know that in 1942 and 1943 David McDonald was sent by the State Department's Latin American Affairs Office (headed by Nelson Rockefeller) to almost all the countries of that continent (Proceedings, Second Constitutional Convention, 228; Kelly 1954, 95).

The USWA was heavily involved in national politics during the war years. Its most visible role was in the CIO's Political Action Committee (PAC) during the 1944 election campaign. The union contributed $100,000 to start PAC in October 1943 and assigned fourteen staff members to the organization full time (Kelly 1954, 83). Though Roosevelt ignored PAC's choice of Henry Wallace for vice president (page 186), the union continued to support the Democratic campaign, and by 1944 about half of all staff time was being spent on the presidential election (page 175).

The success of the union in getting out the votes, like that of PAC in general, was problematic. There are some indications that the USWA may have been particularly effective in mobilizing its members to vote or, just as interesting, that the steelworkers were easier to mobilize. Pittsburgh was the only major city where, compared to 1940, Roosevelt received more votes in 1944 in heavily labor wards than in heavily nonlabor. The Democratic vote in wards of Pittsburgh composed predominantly of steelworkers reached 79 percent, versus 50 percent in white-collar wards. Roosevelt also received 79 percent of the vote in comparable wards in Chicago. Throughout the steel areas, turnout in 1944 was way up (Foster 1975, 208–11). More detailed studies of the voting patterns of workers in steel towns and neighborhoods are needed.

Despite its great importance, we know even less about the role of the union in local and state politics. Steelworkers were the mayors of such towns as Clairton and Duquesne, whose protean mayor, Elmer Malloy, deserving of his own biographical essay, declared June 17 as Philip Murray Day (Proceedings, First Constitutional Convention, 290). And a member of SWOC was elected mayor of Lackawanna in 1941 (*Steel Labor,* March 27, 1942). We need to know much more about not only who was elected in these towns but how much power they wielded and the significance of their elections. It appears that Democratic party victories in these towns meant civil liberties for the union leadership, the elimination of ethnic harassment against Eastern and Southern European lifestyles and institutions, and wholesale incorporation of the "new immigrants" into such organs of the state as the local police forces (Sabadasz 1986, 6; Beaver Valley History Society, Records in Labor Archives, University of Pittsburgh).

A study is also needed to determine what, if any, erosion or growth of union influence occurred during the war at the local level of the Democratic party. When examining the meaning of the new policy, we should note the continued exclusion of blacks from patronage networks and civil rights and of radicals from the civil liberties consensus after the war.

The role of the USWA in local politics in such big cities as Baltimore and Cleveland and, above all, in Chicago and Pittsburgh presents a special problem. Historians have shied away from studies of these cities because of their size and complexity. Studies of the union's role in state politics and the government, at least in Pennsylvania, Illinois, and Ohio, would also yield considerable results.

One final point concerns the role of the union in the changing ecology of the steel towns and neighborhoods. Some striking physical transformations took place. Half the town of Homestead was bulldozed in late 1941 to make way for the expansion of the mill. About nine thousand of the borough's nineteen thousand residents were forced to relocate, as were about twenty-five hundred from Duquesne's Castle Garden neighborhood (Draham, Dougherty, and Marcus; Dickerson 1986, 157). How common were such projects, and what was their impact on the workers and their communities?

We know that the USWA and many of its locals played a major role in the drive for public housing in some areas. The huge Pittsburgh Jones & Laughlin local, 1843, pushed hard and successfully with the city council to obtain local money to match what was available for public housing from the federal government. Once the money was secured, Steve Slavonic, the local's housing director, selected the site for the project and outlined the engineering tasks involved (*Steel Labor,* September 25, 1941). This is not a solitary example.

Most of the new communities were inhabited almost entirely by either white or black steelworkers. What were these new communities like? Did they preserve local traditions and customs while creating solidarity based on proximity and common problems, or were they centers of alienation that furthered the collapse of community, such as the projects depicted in Harriet Arnow's *The Dollmaker?*

One development in many steel towns and neighborhoods was the establishment of substantial new union headquarters, such as the spacious office for Local 1211 in Aliquippa, located in a former bank. It featured two sets of photo murals, one depicting the growth of unionism, the other, the "four freedoms," with the motto "This Building Is A Memorial To Free Speech" (*Steel Labor,* April 28, 1944, 7). Such buildings probably served many community functions. Did lodges and social clubs meet there? Boy and Girl Scouts? More investigation is needed.

One may speculate that the wartime overcrowding and resulting high rents in the steel towns accelerated the postwar drive to the suburbs. This trend does not seem to have been manifest during the war, but the return of the young men, higher wages, and the renewed availability of cheap gasoline and of cars may have been the sparks needed to ignite major community discontent. We know that by 1944 the average steelworker lived six miles from his worksite, whereas only 22 percent still lived within a two-mile radius. We also know that as late as 1944 only 40.6 percent owned or were buying homes (*Steel Labor*, April 28, 1944, 7).

Conclusion

By mid-1946, the USWA and its members had achieved industrial citizenship. They were still far from equal partners in industrial relations or civil society, but they were recognized, grudgingly, as participants in most areas of industrial relations decision making. The very large gains won by and for steelworkers over the next thirty years would build on the progress that had been made from 1939 to 1946.

So too the failure to achieve full industrial democracy during the war would remain the pattern to some extent for the next forty years. Key aspects of industrial tyranny, most notably who would own, manage, and make investment or disinvestment decisions about steelmaking, were left unshaken. The workers and their union are feeling today the tragic consequences of this failure.

This paper has raised many historical questions. In almost all cases, answering them requires considerable research in local union files and corporate personnel records. The most pressing task before all concerned with the accurate depiction of the important and neglected history of SWOC and the USWA is to ensure as much as possible that the union's records are preserved. To that end, I urge that the greatest scholarly priority and support be given to the United Steelworkers of America Archives at Pennsylvania State University and to other such repositories before more of the union's irreplaceable past is destroyed.

Miners escort Murray to a coalfield rally in the 1920s.
Courtesy of the United Steelworkers of America.

The signing of the articles of affiliation between SWOC and the CIO at the first meeting of the Steel Workers' Organizing Committee, on June 17, 1936. David J. McDonald and Phil Murray are flanked at left by officials Joe Gaither and Tom Gillis of the Amalgamated Association of Iron, Steel and Tin Workers, and by Leo Krzycki of the Amalgamated Clothing Workers and Julius Hochman of the International Ladies' Garment Workers on the right. Standing from left are Clinton S. Golden and Van A. Bittner, later vice presidents of the USWA; Pat T. Fagan, UMW official; counsel Lee Pressman; and John Brophy, UMW vice president. Courtesy of the Pennsylvania State University Historical Collections and Labor Archives.

John L. Lewis hands Murray the letter of succession as CIO president, 1940. Courtesy of the United Steelworkers of America.

After the war, it was back to the picket lines in two national steel strikes. Courtesy of the United Steelworkers of America.

Murray campaigned hard for Adlai Stevenson
in 1952, in what turned out to be the last
months of his life. Courtesy of the United
Steelworkers of America.

Murray was an early supporter of Harry S.
Truman when few thought he would win the
1948 presidential election. Courtesy of the
United Steelworkers of America.

BATTLING OVER GOVERNMENT'S ROLE

Ronald W. Schatz

W HAT stands out most clearly about Philip Murray among leaders of labor organizations in North America is that he was one of the earliest and strongest advocates of the idea that the way for industrial unions to survive and advance is to bond themselves with government. I would like to illustrate this point briefly for Murray's years in the mine workers' union and during the New Deal and then show how, after 1946, steel companies and political officials attacked the labor-state relationship that Murray had so carefully helped nurture—foreshadowing the attack directed at the United Steelworkers of America and other unions during the past ten years.

The Need to Steer Clear of Government

Throughout the nineteenth century, most trade unionists and other working-class activists, such as members of cooperative workshops, envisioned their goal and strategy as "the liberation of civil society through economic self-organization," to quote the historian of the Knights of Labor, Leon Fink (1983, 108). The role of the government, from this perspective, was limited, albeit important: essentially to establish and maintain ground rules permitting free labor activity at the local level. For example, when the Workingmen's party came to power in 1878 in the shoe industry town of Lynn, Massachusetts, the only major change

I would like to thank Ilya Vinkovetsky for his research assistance on this paper.

they sought was to remove the police chief, who had been protecting scabs and thereby helping manufacturers break the shoemakers' union (Dawley 1976, 201–02).

The need to steer clear of the federal government was hammered home in 1894 when Grover Cleveland used troops to destroy the boycott of Pullman railroad cars. The leaders of the American Federation of Labor, with their concept of "voluntarism," and the Industrial Workers of the World, with their vision of revolutionary industrial unionism, had this goal, if little else, in common.

In the late nineteenth and early twentieth centuries, however, a broad range of developments occurred that in combination caused AFL leaders to lift their eyes from the local political and economic arenas and begin to pursue their aims through lobbying the U.S. Congress and, after the election of Democrat Woodrow Wilson, the executive branch. Corporations of national and international scope were formed; a growing nationalistic spirit emerged in some labor circles, particularly after the war of 1898; increasingly, injunctions were used against unions during strikes; unionists demanded a total cutoff of immigration from Asia; mediation services were created, first by the National Civic Federation and later by the federal government; and, not least, union leaders began to fear that their organizations would be demolished if they failed to cooperate with the federal government during mobilization for war.

On the eve of the U.S. entry into the First World War, Samuel Gompers joined the advisory commission of the Council of National Defense, a committee created to maintain war production, increase productivity, and, as far as Gompers was concerned, protect existing wage standards. As part of the same process or trend, new, younger union figures emerged, men such as Sidney Hillman, who espoused industrial unionism, industrial cooperation, and union participation in national politics (see Taft 1957, chaps. 18–23; Montgomery 1979, chap. 3; Tomlins 1985, 71–77ff; Conner 1983, 20–22; Fraser 1983, 212–55).

Philip Murray was outstanding among these men. Appointed to the International Executive Board of the United Mine Workers in 1912 at the age of only twenty-nine, the soft-spoken, skillful young negotiator became president of the UMW's rapidly expanding western Pennsylvania district three years later. When the United States entered the war in Europe, Murray was appointed to two new federal agencies: the National Bituminous Coal Production Committee and the Pennsylvania Regional War Labor Board. Thus, at virtually the beginning of his career Philip Murray was enmeshed in forwarding the interests of workers and unions through federal channels. Indeed, two of Murray's mentors in the UMW—the district president for western Pennsylvania, Francis Feehan, and the union's International president, John P. White, left the union in these years to become government officials in the labor relations field (Tate 1962, 18–19; Cooke and Murray 1940, vii; Dubofsky and Van Tine 1977, 37; "Brief Biography of Francis Feehan").

Establishing a Union-Government Alliance

From the beginning of the First World War through V-J Day, Philip Murray consistently supported the formation of an alliance between industrial unions and the government in Washington. On one hand, he would argue that semiskilled workers such as those he represented needed federal support to overcome the opposition of companies; on the other, that labor organizations would be crushed if they lined up against Washington on such sensitive matters as wartime strikes and United States foreign policy.

In November 1919, for example, UMW leaders terminated a two-week-old national bituminous strike in the face of a sweeping federal injunction, federal plans to provide one hundred thousand troops to protect strikebreakers, a declaration of martial law in the coal-producing state of Wyoming, and a promise to create a presidential commission to award wage increases. When UMW convention delegates reconvened in 1920 to consider the matter, it was district president Murray who offered the resolution in defense of the leaders' conduct. "My friends, these are stern, real, cold facts that no body can hope to get away from," he warned. "When I made the motion that we . . . endorse the policy they have pursued, I did it with the feeling deep in my heart that it was the only course for the coal miners to pursue under present day circumstances. There isn't a delegate in this convention who wants to . . . array the forces of his local union against the most powerful and strongly organized government in the world" (Proceedings, 24).

The other side of Murray's position was illustrated two years later, in 1921, when twenty thousand coal miners, bearing arms and commanded by war veterans, defied machine-gun fire and bombing by light planes to march on Logan County, West Virginia, in an attempt to overturn company dictatorship. At the request of President Warren Harding, Murray hurried to Logan County to urge the miners to go home, yet subsequently he told the U.S. Senate Committee on Education and Labor that the report of the Bituminous Coal Commission, the committee that had settled the 1919 strike, should apply to nonunion coal operators as much as to UMW-organized companies. "During the period of the strike," he maintained, "the Government did not hesitate to use its great authority, under the war powers, against the United Mine Workers, even to the extent of placing its members in jail. Is there any reason why it should not have used its authority, under the same war powers, to make the non-union operators observe the terms of a decision by a government tribunal?" (Murray 1921, 42–43ff).

Murray told the senators that if the Harding administration failed to act, they themselves should draw up an agreement, require the operators and the UMW to sign, and ask the chief justice of the Supreme Court to appoint an arbitrator who, in Murray's words, "will interpret and apply the agreement and pass upon grievances." Neither Harding nor the senators complied, of course, given the politics of the era, but in the late 1940s, after the industrial unions had built up massive power, Harry Truman would adopt an approach to steel conflicts similar to the one Murray had proposed a quarter-century before (Murray 1921, 42–43ff; Tate 1962, 29).

During the 1930s Murray's commitment to working through an alliance with the federal government intensified. This commitment took the form of offering unquestioning support for Franklin Roosevelt. While John L. Lewis stood as the official head of a labor-support committee for the reelection of President Herbert Hoover in 1932, Murray led a group of six UMW leaders to meet with the New York governor. Sitting at ease at the end of a long divan in the governor's mansion in Albany, Roosevelt told the unionists that he knew something of the miners' travails, for his family had earlier owned stock in Pennsylvania coal firms. If elected president, Roosevelt promised, he would use his authority to bring the coal operators to a collective bargaining agreement with the UMW (McDonald 1969, 67–68). The National Industrial Recovery Act, enacted in 1933, embodied the tripartism Murray had been calling for in the 1920s (Hawley 1966, 119). Murray and Lewis, of course, poured hundreds of thousands of union members' dollars into the reelection of Roosevelt in 1936. But when Lewis endorsed Republican candidate Wendell Willkie on the eve of the 1940 presidential election, Murray defied his mentor and remained true to Roosevelt. As CIO director of organization, John Brophy, later explained: "Murray was in the position of having the job of organizing steel which had not been completed. . . . Murray was conscious of the fact that he would need to maintain friendly relations with the Administration" (Oral history transcript, Brophy Papers, 860–61).

Murray's steadfastness to Washington provoked intense criticism from both right and left over the years. "My belief in the trade-union movement in America is such that I don't think we should have a trade-union movement unless that movement is prepared to render a service to its people and to its country," he told the November 1942 CIO convention, adding, "There are no qualifications attached to that statement; there never has been and, insofar as I am personally concerned, there is not going to be. I am determined to support our Commander-in-Chief and I am going to support him" (Proceedings, 12–15). A year earlier he had declared, "I have never quibbled about my attitude in the field of national defense" (Proceedings, 12). Ultimately, Murray's commitment led to his break with John Lewis in the winter of 1941, a fissure not only deeply painful to both men personally—each subsequently suffered a heart attack—but terribly damaging to the labor movement, for it foreclosed essential cooperation between the unions they led.

But without the backing of the federal government it is very doubtful that the UMW, which had lost most of its membership and contracts at the nadir of the Depression, could have revived as rapidly as it did in 1933 and 1934, that the Steel Workers' Organizing Committee would have been able by 1942 to secure contracts from such violently anti-union firms as Republic Steel, or that the CIO, far weaker than any outsider knew when Murray assumed its presidency in 1940, would have reached its mammoth size by V-J Day.

A Plan to Strengthen the Bond

Philip Murray had greater hopes. In 1941 he put forward his now-famous industrial councils plan for guiding the United States economy during World War II. Drawing on Pope Pius XI's encyclical *Quadragesimo Anno* and his personal experiences with tripartite boards during World War I and the early New Deal era (when he was briefly codirector of the National Recovery Administration), Murray proposed for each industry the formation of councils consisting of equal numbers of labor and corporate representatives and chaired by a federal official. The councils would determine market needs, allocate orders, schedule plant expansion and production, determine priorities, and establish labor policies. In addition, there would be "a central policy-making and coordinating board," also composed of equal numbers of labor and management representatives, staffed by federal officials, and chaired by the president of the United States. This board would make general allocations to the industrial councils and handle all other economic matters "not handled by the industry councils, as for example, government housing, health and welfare activities and protection of the general consumer interest" (Brophy Papers, "1941, CIO—B-J"; Schatz 1981).

It was hardly surprising that business leaders rejected the plan. Murray's councils would have given labor leaders status and power equal to that of management, in fact higher, by organizing economic planning on the basis of whole industries rather than separate corporations. More disturbing, the plan was dismissed by Roosevelt and his aides, who had always been concerned about corporate attitudes and at that time were wooing business support for war mobilization. "Labor's chief difficulty in America today, as in days gone by, lies in the unwillingness, the obvious unwillingness of government and business to accept labor in good faith," Philip Murray protested in November 1941 (CIO Proceedings, 320). "Why should the agencies of government in Washington today be virtually infested with wealthy men, men who are supposedly receiving one dollar a year compensation?" he demanded in 1942. "What are we running?" he shouted, "a war production organization to win the war, or a war production organization to destroy labor?" (Proceedings, 14–15).

"Sinful Legislation"

Anti-union fervor heated during the mid-1940s, stirred by resentment of the wartime coal strikes Lewis had led, by the huge immediate postwar walkouts in steel, auto, electrical goods, coal, and the railroads, and by the inflation of consumer prices following the lifting of wartime price controls. Businesses purposely intensified antilabor feelings by announcing increases in prices immediately after wage settlements, a tactic that succeeded in making the unions seem wholly responsible.

In the spring of 1947, the majority of state legislatures passed laws sharply constraining labor organization and activity, and most other states were debating such measures. Some states banned sitdown strikes, jurisdictional strikes, slowdowns, or mass picketing. (Mass picketing was described in Texas as three union members per plant gate!) Some states forbade strikes in hospitals, public utilities, state government, or on farms. Others prohibited closed-shop or union-shop contracts. Still others outlawed secondary boycotts, made unions just as subject to "unfair labor practice" charges as employers, or required ratification of strike calls by secret ballot. This list is far from complete (see *Business Week,* February 1, April 5, May 17, and especially June 14, 1947).

The Taft-Hartley Act, passed by Congress in June 1947, was the culmination of the larger postwar political effort to sever the ties tentatively established during the New Deal between labor unions and the government. Under the law, bans on union activity, previously enacted only in states where labor organizations were weak, were now invoked across the nation. In addition, the law blocked the door of the National Labor Relations Board to any union whose officers refused to sign affidavits that they were not Communists—a move that opened up unions such as the United Electrical, Radio and Machine Workers (UE) to raiding by others, such as the United Auto Workers, the majority of whose leaders were happy to sign such affidavits. The legislation also prevented unions from contributing directly to political campaigns, as Lewis and Murray had done in 1936 so to create a setting suitable for building SWOC. Most troubling to Philip Murray, however, given the continental character of bargaining in the steel industry, was the revival in the law of the use of federal injunctions against strikes and the establishment of a "cooling-off period" in "national emergencies." (For further discussion of Murray's views, see CIO Proceedings 1947, 18–28.)

A man apt to reach for religious metaphors in times of crisis, Philip Murray characterized the law as the work of the devil. Standing before the October 1947 CIO convention, he said:

> The Taft-Hartley bill was conceived in sin; that it was a sinful piece of legislation, and that its promoters were diabolical men who, seething with hatred, . . . contrived this ugly measure for the purpose of imposing their wrath upon the millions of . . . workers. . . . The Wagner Act [was] brought into being in the United States in the year of 1935 . . . as a measure designed to give to American workers their economic freedom . . . to exercise their God-given right to vote for that union if they wanted to. . . . The Wagner Act never interfered with collective bargaining. . . . But along comes the Taft-Hartley Act, and . . . [it] sets up some commandments, some things which in substance say to the employers and workers, "Thou shall not do." (Proceedings 1947, 22)

Six months later, at the Steelworkers' convention, he recalled for the delegates the history of the Norris-LaGuardia anti-injunction act, passed in 1932 but now effectively repealed. "The Act . . . grew out of the manifold industrial disputes . . . many years ago when the coal and iron police and the deputy sheriffs and the state and county and Federal Courts were put to use to bludgeon, to murder, to imprison, to incarcerate and beat up the workers engaged in strike. . . .

"I fought for that legislation in the halls of Congress, . . ." Murray told his members, "and for a period . . . American labor was comparatively free as far as the use of the injunctive process against them. . . . But along came the Taft-Hartley Act with all its repressions and all of its oppressions. . . . The courts are now being used in almost every instance, the strong, mighty arm of the Federal Government, to repress labor." Perhaps trying even still to extend a hand to John Lewis, he added, "That was particularly noticeable in the recent Mine Workers' situation" (USWA Proceedings 1948, 195–96).

As before, Murray's response to a labor crisis was political, but the character of the political goals and modes was different now. In the long period between the administrations of Wilson and of Roosevelt, Murray had urged the establishment of such tripartite systems as industrial councils, which would have intentionally and inevitably increased the membership and strength of the unions he led. After 1946, when the United Steelworkers and other CIO unions were large and powerful, he simply sought to defend the link between unions and the federal government— and, more particularly, because the majority of the Congress was hostile, the bond with the president—on which their strength rested.

The first steps toward strengthening this bond were to revive the Political Action Committee, a branch of the CIO Murray and Sidney Hillman had created in 1944 to stave off the growth of labor parties developing in Akron and other union towns, and to reelect Franklin Roosevelt. Murray's new goal was to kick out antilabor congressmen elected in the wake of the 1946 strikes, prepare for the next presidential campaign, and repeal the Taft-Hartley bill. "We are undertaking for the first time in our history a real national organization to organize votes, and to get out large registrations. Every unit affiliated with the national CIO is now bending every possible effort toward the accomplishment of that objective, namely, the largest registration we have ever had in the history of our Nation, for the year 1948. It is the only way these problems can be answered," he told the CIO delegates in mid-October 1947 (Proceedings, 24). "Men of steel, you mighty legions of labor, . . . one of the mightiest labor organizations in the entire world, close your ranks," he implored the delegates, making their work synonymous with virility, "cease divisions— and there isn't much of that in steel, thank God," he added, alluding to the virtual exclusion of Communists from his union. "Devote your time and your energies on this political and leg- islative front . . . give it your dollars . . . fight them out on the political battlefield" (USWA Proceedings 1948, 197).

At the same time, Murray reconsidered his positions regarding the role of Communists in the labor movement and on President Harry Truman. Philip Murray had long hated "Russianized rev- olution," as he called it at the mine workers' convention in 1924. Yet he was willing to compromise when necessary, and he and Lewis had employed supporters of the Communist party on the staff of SWOC in the late 1930s and had cooperated with left- wing unionists not only during the war but in postwar politicking. Murray had opposed the Democrats' choice of Truman for vice president in 1944, even though he had no viable alternative and Roosevelt had indicated a strong preference for the politically centrist Missourian. After the war, Philip Murray was one of the most prominent members of the Progressive Citizens of America, a group of liberals, left-wingers, and Communists dissatisfied with Truman and looking for a different Democratic presidential nominee for the next election or, in some cases, for a new political party altogether.

Despite his personal feelings, Murray thought that the enact- ment of Taft-Hartley made the Steelworkers more dependent than ever on the goodwill of the president. CIO officials sensitive to the Communist party ignored Murray's concern and chose to back and staff former vice president Henry Wallace and the new Progressive party for president. To Murray, this action was rea- son enough to eliminate these officials from the CIO. So, in 1948 he replaced Lee Pressman, a left-wing attorney with whom he had been close, with Arthur Goldberg, an equally smart but strictly anti-Communist lawyer, and with Goldberg's help coun- tenanced the indictment and expulsion of ten left-wing unions from the CIO. (For more on Murray's reluctance to support Truman, both in 1944 and 1948, see McDonald 1969, 170–72 and 193–97. On Murray's approach to CIO leaders allied with the Communist party, see Goldberg 1956, 177–85, and Levenstein 1981, chaps. 9–17.)

Postwar Strikes Paralyze the Industry

The United Steelworkers of America and the large steel corporations engaged in highly publicized contractual disputes every year between 1946 and 1952. Canadian and United States steelworkers struck three times in this brief period: in 1946, 1949, and 1952. The strikes were enormous, the largest by any union in the history of North America. The controversies were so sharply focused, orchestrated, and, as time went by, hard fought that newspaper reporters wrote about them as boxing matches: round one, round two, round three. . . .

Given the lack of violence, however, compared to the steel strikes of 1919 and 1937 and that in monetary terms the strikes were ultimately over small amounts—three cents per hour the first time—outside, middle-class observers tended to think that the conflicts were unimportant, unnecessary, and even trivial. Historians have tended to perpetuate this interpretation. One widely read historian, Thomas Brooks, described the sides in the 1946 strike as "friendly warriors" (1971, chap. 16). This epithet does not convey an adequate understanding of the strike of January 1946 and definitely not those afterward.

The union desired, first, to make up for the large drop in earnings suffered by workers in 1945–46, now that they were no longer receiving overtime pay and government price controls had been lifted (USWA Proceedings 1946, 118–21; Schatz 1983, 151–57). The union's drive was intensified by the personal competition between Murray and the leaders of the United Auto Workers and the United Electrical, Radio and Machine Workers. Which CIO union leader would secure the best contracts—Phil Murray? His extremely aggressive young rival, Walter Reuther? Or "the Reds"? Of equal or greater importance on the labor side was the desire to obtain pensions for its older members. Because the steel industry had expanded immensely between 1914 and 1923, a giant cohort of men was nearing retirement age by the late 1940s. The social security system had been created in the late 1930s, but payments were not sufficient to support retired workers. Company officials enjoyed private pensions; the union demanded them for workers too (CIO Proceedings 1948, 56–57; CIO Proceedings 1949, 230; USWA Proceedings 1948, 158–63; Durand 1948, 33–46, 110–16, 123–24, 184–86).

Steel companies, in turn, had two large grievances. First, they felt that management had been "penetrated" by the union and workers, to use the words of the industrial relations authority at the time, Neil Chamberlain (1946, chap. 4). Second, they believed that they had lost power to the union in general and to Philip Murray in particular.

Since at least 1937, when the Roosevelt administration had recommended widespread price reductions in steel to stimulate consumer purchasing power, people in Washington had been "snapping at the heels" of the steel companies. First the government pushed the companies to cut prices; then it denied them price increases considered essential by management; later it leaned heavily on companies to increase steel capacity. On two occasions in 1946 Truman called Murray and the head of U.S. Steel, Benjamin Fairless, into his office, and in 1949 and 1951 he formed "fact-finding boards" to specify wage increases (Spencer 1955, 33–38). No one else was being targeted this way, steel officials felt. Their feelings were not unjustified, for in the mid-twentieth century the steel industry was considered by everyone relevant—economists, labor leaders, and the public—to be the linchpin of all industry. As Clarence B. Randall, president of Inland Steel of East Chicago, Indiana, said pithily in 1952, "We goose-step to the music of Pittsburgh" (1952, 34; see also *Business Week*, January 15 and September 3, 1949; Spencer 1955, 3–7; and U.S. Department of Labor 1961, 5). In Britain, the socialist government was nationalizing steel. Was that in store for America? company heads asked. "Who Shall Plan, You or Uncle Sam?" cried the industry's weekly, *Iron Age*, on November 11, 1946, the eve of the congressional elections. To a few, Murray seemed like a socialist (see also *Business Week*, September 3, 1949, 88).

This concentration on government separates the postwar battles from the pre–World War II strikes and explains the qualities that seemed strange to observers at the time. There was no violence, for example, because the companies, having accepted the existence of the union, had no reason to break lines around factories. The line they were trying to break ran between union headquarters in Pittsburgh and the Oval Office. Lawyers and public-relations experts rather than scabs were needed for that job. Later, during the Carter years and the early period of the Reagan administration, labor organizers pinpointed company-employed legal firms as the primary agents of union busting. That strategy originated in the 1940s in steel.

"The Steelworkers Respected the Rules"

In 1952 the steel companies launched an all-out attack on the alliance between Murray, the steelworkers, and the White House. Leading figures in the industry openly diagnosed the problem. "It appears that we are on the eve of another election year and that some of our political leaders, and certain pressure groups, are clearly attempting once again to make American industry their whipping boy, . . ." Ben Fairless, president of U.S. Steel, declared on the fifteenth of November 1951, the day the steel-workers' union announced its twenty-two new contract demands. "The negotiations . . . involve broad questions of public policy which go beyond the scope of collective bargaining in these days of wage and price control. For my purposes . . . the important fact is that labor has possessed the economic and political power to enforce its demands" (see Spencer 1955, 138–39).

Although Truman repeatedly used Taft-Hartley injunctions against John L. Lewis's mine workers, he adopted a different course, somewhat more favorable to labor, regarding CIO unions, particularly the Steelworkers. Randall of Inland Steel put it this way: "The procedure is quite simple. While an emergency is on, the union announces a paralyzing strike in a basic industry, and then the day before the catastrophe hits, graciously stands aside to permit men from outside who bear no responsibility for its welfare to determine what is best for it." Randall continued:

> The sequence is always substantially the same before a fact-finding board. Unions never lose. Of course, they don't get all of their demands, but they always get something. . . . Among the factors that influence the decisions of public members of fact-finding

boards let no one underestimate the importance of . . . their unwillingness to let an important labor personality lose face. It is
known in management circles as the "Phil has got to have something" principle. . . . I have heard it in I can't tell how many
government conferences. (1952, 39–40)

Corporate strategy followed logically from this analysis. The
manufacturers made no response at all to the twenty-two demands issued by the Steelworkers in November 1951. Their
reasoning was that since the authorities would pick final terms
partway between the positions of the union and the companies,
it made no sense to volunteer concessions. To ensure that production was not interrupted for the war in Korea, Truman appointed a Wage Stabilization Board to consider the dispute. The
companies demanded unacceptably high price increases all the
time the board was meeting, and then, when the board's report
was issued, rejected its recommendations.

Truman seized the mills to avert a strike, rightly blaming the
manufacturers for the impasse, but the companies screamed that
he was abusing his power and secured a federal district court
order and a Supreme Court decision invalidating the president's
actions. The companies then took a strike—the longest in the
steel industry since 1919—and withheld settlement until the
twenty-fourth of July, the very day the Democratic National
Convention nominated Illinois governor Adlai Stevenson for
president.

Throughout the seven-month-long dispute, Philip Murray
railed at the companies' unwillingness to play by the government's rules. "The nation has its rules," he told the May 1952
Steelworkers' convention. "The Steelworkers in this situation re-
spected the rules adopted for their guidance by the Government.
The steel industry has not." Enraged by the manufacturers' de-
fiance of Washington, Murray resorted to language uncharac-
teristic of him in public: "The Wage Stabilization Board has
already compromised your situation; it has given you much less
than you hoped to get through collective bargaining. You protest
the decision . . . but accept it in the national interest, and then
the steel industry comes along and it says . . . 'Oh, no, we don't
bargain with you on that basis, we are just meeting with you for

the purpose of taking something away from you,' and I say to them, 'Go to hell' " (USWA Proceedings 1952, 13–15).

The hard line taken by the steel companies in the 1952 negotiations made clear the limitations of the strategy for building labor power that Philip Murray and other industrial unionists had been pursuing since the Wilson era. Harry Truman did everything possible, including seizing the steel mills, to make the manufacturers heel. He failed. The ultimate terms of the steel contract were satisfactory to Murray, but by the time the union and company had settled, the Truman administration was so weakened that the Republicans had gained their first real chance to capture the White House since FDR's election in 1932.

Historians do not ordinarily consider Dwight Eisenhower's 1952 presidential election a watershed, but to Philip Murray it was a frightening prospect, for, unlike Truman, Eisenhower was unencumbered by obligations to organized labor. Instead, he was indebted to Senator Robert Taft, leader of the Republican party and author of the Taft-Hartley Act. As the astute political commentator Samuel Lubell wrote at the time:

> Many labor leaders are painfully aware that much of their following was recruited under the patronage of a friendly government, rather than through labor's own strength. What if an unsympathetic administration came to power? What if that coincided with a recession? *The still unexploded dynamite of . . . Taft-Hartley . . . lies in those fears. . . . The real threat in the act lies in its union-busting power during a period of unemployment, when labor's bargaining power is weak, and a government hostile to labor might be in power.* (1965, 178; emphasis added)

Exhausted by the long battle over the steel contract, worried about the possibility of suffering a coronary as he had ten years earlier, and forbidden by his doctor from traveling on an airplane, Murray, then sixty-six years old, courageously crisscrossed the country by train, warning union members of a "raw deal," "vicious, dangerous amendments to the Taft-Hartley Act," and a "blitzkrieg against labor" if Stevenson was defeated (*Steel Labor*, November 1952, 1–2). Eisenhower's landslide victory was "one of the biggest defeats[,] one of his saddest moments," recalled James Malone, Murray's nephew and a Steelworkers staff member, who was beside him when the returns came in. "That was a very hard blow to him. Because he banked everything on that. . . . The whole structure as far as he was concerned was depending on Adlai Stevenson becoming President of the United States" (personal interview, October 19, 1983; McDonald 1969, 226). "That was hard, that was hard," remembered Murray's son, Joseph. "I think it broke his heart. I think it broke his heart" (personal interview).

The morning after the election, Murray boarded a train for California, where he was to preside over the CIO's fourteenth constitutional convention. He died four days later.

COMMENTS

I. W. ABEL

I. W. Abel was active in SWOC and the USWA during its early years as a local union officer, district director in Ohio, and International secretary-treasurer and was president of the union from 1965 to 1977. These comments were made at his last public appearance before he died on August 10, 1987.

I was a bit disturbed by the title of one of our presentations, "Labor's Odd Couple." I don't think either John Lewis or Phil Murray was odd, and I don't think they were completely opposites by any stretch of the imagination. But I think they complemented each other. I am confident that without John Lewis heading the CIO it never would have gotten off the ground. John Lewis played the devil's advocate and then, after things reached a certain stage, Phil Murray, the compromiser, would move onto the scene and accomplish what both of them had agreed to do in the first place.

Lewis and Murray were a working team. On many occasions, as president and vice president of the United Mine Workers, John Lewis stirred up the storm and Phil Murray came in and pacified the waters and achieved the settlements that were necessary. As an example, one of the last acts Phil Murray did before he departed, not of his own will, from the Mine Workers was to go in during the coal strike of 1941 and negotiate and successfully secure a union shop for the United Mine Workers of America.

I recall well the days, weeks, and months leading up to Phil Murray's expulsion from the United Mine Workers. His expulsion had a lot to do not just with personalities but with the posture of the country and the world situation in the period before the war. John had certain set views, and Phil Murray had strong personal loyalties and was a very strong supporter of his government. They came to a parting of the ways when Lewis felt called upon to endorse Wendell Willkie and Murray, the next day, issued the position of the CIO in support of President Roosevelt.

In Lewis's famous radio address endorsing Willkie, he said to the members of the CIO in particular, but I think he was talking to all of labor, "Uphold me now or repudiate me. If you repudiate me, you'll have to have a new president of the CIO at the next convention because I will retire." Of course, he was repudiated, and in spite of efforts to change his mind, Lewis retired at the Atlantic City convention and Murray was elected president. From that time until his expulsion from the Mine Workers, Murray called many meetings of our executive board solely for the purpose of letting us know what was taking place and how it affected him personally.

It was a devastation to Murray to break with Lewis and to be expelled from the United Mine Workers. In the years that followed their falling out, they didn't speak to each other. There were differences between them, but certainly they were not oddballs, and I think the labor movement is much better off today because we had the two of them, because they did so complement each other.

Let me move now to our early days in steel. I was fortunate to be in on the ground floor. As was pointed out, the Steelworkers' agreement with Timken was signed on April 7, 1937, and the following June we got involved in the so-called Little Steel strike. I've been a little disturbed that several speakers referred to the *devastated* Little Steel strike, to what a total defeat it was. I take issue with that. The Little Steel strike was not a disaster. It has provided many benefits for us down through the years. True, the strike was lost, but only after eighteen months. I don't know how many appreciate what it was like to be on strike for eighteen months, to be beaten up and arrested by local police, to be put in jail and to have the National Guard called out and used against you, to see fellow strikers shot down like animals and still wage the battle. Only after eighteen months did the union call off the strike. But because it was called off does not mean that it was a defeat, not by any stretch of the imagination. I remind you that the union petitioned the National Labor Relations Board and that after extensive hearings Republic Steel was ordered to reinstate all the strikers they had refused to take back and had blackballed and to pay them their lost wages for that time period. Many of them received substantial back-pay checks.

In addition, during the famous LaFollette investigation, the spotlight was turned to industry in general and to the steel industry in particular, to their ruthlessness toward their workers and the fact that they had within their plants and their properties larger gestapos and armies than most communities. They had arsenals beyond imagination; they revealed how the corporations controlled our local police, how they controlled the sheriffs' offices, and, of course, how they controlled the governor of the state of Ohio, who used the troops against us. I think it's significant that since the revelations of the LaFollette investigation, the steel industry has been very careful not to keep arms or armed police in great numbers on their properties or to use such force to stop a strike. In the many strikes since 1937 and the LaFollette investigation, steel companies have never once opened their plant gates and attempted to scab their operations.

To me, those are great victories. They are lasting victories. One other observation. Although the strikers in a sense were unorganized during the Little Steel strike, they exercised political muscle through Labor's Non-Partisan League. We retired the governor of Ohio, Martin Davey, to private life and put an end to his ambitions for a political career.

Another benefit of the Little Steel strike is that in all those years, the National Guard has never been used to put down steel strikers, and we've had some pretty long and bitter strikes. So you see, it wasn't a lost cause completely. We may have failed to get an agreement at the time, but, even though the strike was called off, the company recognized representatives of our workers, members filed grievances, local union officers and staff representatives of our union met with company personnel people and managers and negotiated settlements for those grievances. We continued to make efforts to bargain, and eventually, in 1941, we signed an agreement with Republic Steel and the rest of the Little Steel industry followed along the line. So you see, it's not, in my judgment, appropriate to refer to the Little Steel strike as a disaster, as something neither Philip Murray nor the Steelworkers should have gotten themselves involved in.

Another point also calls for clarification. Reference was made to the backwardness or slowness of the Steelworkers to integrate or accept black workers as members in the union and to give them representation. I refer again to the Mine Workers. When defining eligibility for membership, the Mine Workers' constitution and our constitution were identical. Both provide that all members working in and around the mill, the plant, the mine, or an operation shall be eligible for membership in the union irrespective of race, creed, color, or national origin. That's the way it has always been in the Mine Workers and in the Steelworkers. True, the entire membership employed in the steel industry, as in all other industries, did not immediately embrace that philosophy and that policy, and I suppose there are still people in the steel mills, as well as in the coal mines, who have their prejudices and resist accepting a black worker or a female worker on the job or as members of their union. But the policy of the union was the policy of Phil Murray and Dave McDonald and Clint Golden and everybody else, and it was enforced.

While I was director of our district in Canton, Ohio, during World War II, President Roosevelt, in order to avail our nation of the contributions of all workers, felt called upon to issue an executive order, called 8802, which said to industry, "You must hire all workers, regardless of race, creed, or color." It so happened that 80 percent of the workers in the Timken plant that I came out of were from North and South Carolina, Tennessee, and Georgia. When Roosevelt issued his executive order, the Timken Company, being anti-Roosevelt and anti-New Deal, went out on the streets and hired fifty black workers, took them into the plant, and put them in top jobs. You can imagine what took place. Those fellows from the Carolinas, Tennessee, and Georgia ran them out with lead hammers and pieces of pipe. The battle raged for six weeks. All our efforts failed. At that point, President Murray said, "There's only one way left, and that's for me to revoke the charter of that local union and designate you as administrator. You, then, as administrator exercise your authority to remove your membership from the union and under our agreement make the membership insist that the company remove those fellows from the payroll." This we did. We settled the strike, the fellows took us to court, and six months later we got a judgment against us and had to pay them for their lost pay. It settled the strike though, and it enforced the executive order of the president of the United States.

Since then, the commitment of the United Steelworkers to all workers regardless of their race, creed, or color has expanded, of course. I was privileged to appoint a black member as vice president, and many, many more blacks are now in top positions in the International office and, of course, at the local level.

WALTER BURKE

Walter Burke was active as a local and district official during the early years of SWOC and the USWA. He was the elected director in Wisconsin and northwest Illinois for a decade and the secretary-treasurer of the union from 1965 to 1977.

I never had the privilege of knowing Phil Murray so intimately that it could be said I walked so closely in his shadow that if he stopped suddenly I would trip over him. My first real exposure to Phil was in 1942, when as a staff man I was asked by my director to attend a meeting in Pittsburgh that Phil Murray had called for a very specific purpose.

In 1942 one of the perennial matters before the War Labor Board was how to redress the wage inequities in the basic steel industry. It was one of the most bothersome and pesky problems that the USWA had in its relations with the industry and with its own members. The inequities were grievous, membership dissatisfaction was rampant, and while time after time our negotiations had achieved a great deal, they never achieved redress to the inequity problem. Much to everybody's surprise, in 1942 the War Labor Board did address the matter of wage inequities and directed the companies to allot up to five cents per hour per person for this purpose. Little did we realize, initially, how inadequate that amount of money was. Phil Murray, frankly, didn't know what to do about it, so he went to the directors and said, "Anybody on your district staff who has had experience in negotiating the elimination of wage inequalities and has been able to secure some redress to them, I'd like to have come in and meet with me for a couple of days in Pittsburgh. We have a problem to solve."

I had been involved in my district in what was known in the trade as "job evaluation" programs, and we had used the National Electrical Manufacturers Association (NEMA) manual to work out some of the problems relative to the existing wage inequities. I was the only district staff representative who had that experience, and I was delegated to go to Pittsburgh and meet with Mr. Murray and thirty to thirty-five other staff members with varying degrees of similar experience. We talked the problem over for two or three days. I was younger and brasher then, and

I had a pretty big mouth, and I got up and expounded on various ways to tackle the problem of wage inequities. It became very, very evident early in the discussions that Mr. Murray had no time for job evaluation as such. He called it mumbo-jumbo hocus-pocus and said that he wanted no part of it in his union. So we learned, after the first morning's session, that we shouldn't mention job evaluation by name, but we talked around it nevertheless.

After about two and a half days of meetings, Phil Murray said to all of us, "Gentlemen, I've heard enough. I've made a decision. I'm appointing a committee to assist our negotiating committee with this problem in the basic steel industry." Then I learned, to my horror, that he had already written down names. So he pointed his finger and said, "You and you and you and you are now on the committee." I was one of the "yous." So, what started out to be a three- or four-day meeting in Pittsburgh turned out to be about a three-and-a-half-year meeting. It wasn't until three and a half years later that I returned to my district, and then only because the director had passed away rather suddenly and Mr. Murray decided to designate me as the acting director. Otherwise I would probably have stayed on the Wage Inequity Committee for another year or so.

We had some interesting experiences during that three and a half years. Mr. Murray summoned us to his office at least once a week and sometimes more often. Every meeting opened with a question, "Have you gotten me my nickel?" We tried to explain that this undertaking wasn't the easiest task in the world. I've often suspected, although he never said so, that after a couple of weeks, Phil Murray would gladly have accepted the nickel across the board and postponed the matter of eliminating wage inequities for another negotiation. He never said that, but he kept asking for his nickel and couldn't understand why we didn't have an agreement on it.

I can recall very distinctly one day when I thought I would deign to enlighten Mr. Murray as to what the problem was, so I cleared my throat and said, "Mr. Murray, let me try to give you an illustration. You know, when you erect a building, you first have to pour the concrete foundation. Then you erect the steel structure of that building, and after the steel structure is up you begin to lay in steel plates and bricks and mortar. Each operation is interdependent upon the other; you can't lay bricks and mortar before you have the concrete foundation or the steel structure." He listened very politely, but there was a certain look in his eye, and when I ground to a halt, he said, "Is that all, Walter?" I said, "Yes." "Well," he said, "Walter, my boy, you're a perfectionist, and a perfectionist is often an obstructionist. Now, I want to say to you as clearly as I know how today, 'Pour me no concrete, erect me no steel structure, lay up no bricks and mortar. Get me my nickel!' " That ended all the high-level technological discussions as far as job evaluation as a proper redress to wage inequities was concerned.

In effect, we ended up with a job evaluation program, but we developed our own manual. The charm of doing that was that our manual was weighted differently than any of the others in existence. The NEMA manual and several others were weighted heavily toward skills. Of course, when you heavily weight the skills in a mass-production industry like steel, the machinists and roll turners and electricians and others in high-level jobs come out very well. They have skills; they have to serve apprenticeships and so on. But the poor guy out in the mill who works his heart and his life out producing the product the company profits from can't get very much above the minimum wage. This was the problem with all the existing manuals. So with great difficulty and much travail, we prevailed upon the steel industry to develop the Cooperative Wage Study (CWS) manual, which was weighted heavily toward "responsibility" factors. That manual did an excellent job as far as the wage structure in the steel industry was concerned. Phil Murray accepted it; he commended us for it. We never called it a "job evaluation" program; we called it a Cooperative Wage Study. On that basis, we got on quite well with Mr. Murray, and, as I said, he was more than satisfied with the result.

Ronald Schatz reported in his paper that Jimmy Malone, Phil Murray's nephew, described Murray's reaction when Adlai Stevenson was plowed under by General Eisenhower. Malone, as I understood Professor Schatz, said that it probably broke Phil's heart and that four days later he was dead. I am one of the individuals still living who happened to be in San Francisco the night Phil Murray passed away. His last official act on earth, as far as I know, was to address a banquet that was the culminating event of a district conference run by director Charlie Smith. Phil Murray was the guest of honor at the banquet, and as the speaker of the evening, he did an exceptionally admirable job. All of Phil Murray's speeches, as far as I'm concerned, were admirable. When he spoke, you hung on every word. He was indeed a great orator.

That night he talked about the reverses we had just suffered in the political field, but he didn't talk as a broken-hearted man. He talked as a man who had laid himself down to bleed a bit but who was certainly ready to rise and fight again. He was full of plans for the future. He talked about leaving the next day for the CIO convention in Los Angeles, where we would address some of these problems and develop a mechanism to make sure that what had just happened to us politically didn't happen again. He was anything but broken-hearted! He talked about one of his favorite subjects—our responsibility to the membership we represented. He said that our dedication must run to providing a place for each member with a picture on the wall, a carpet on the floor, and music in the home. That was one of Phil Murray's favorite themes, and he meant every word of it; it wasn't just rhetoric.

I went up to him after his speech, as he was leaving the banquet hall, and told him that I certainly enjoyed his remarks, and he said, "Good, Walter. You are going down to Los Angeles, aren't you?" I said, "Yes." He said, "Well, good, we have our work cut out for us, and I'm sure we'll be able to work out our problems. Good night." The next morning I learned to my horror that he had passed away during the night.

Phil Murray was the kind of man who could talk to the entire staff of the Steelworkers, as I heard him do on one occasion, and, in his own inimitable way, dress them down a little bit and yet have them leave the meeting determined as never before to go out and "do it for the old man." That comes pretty close to a phrase that you hear lately, "Let's do it for the Gipper." In Phil's case it was, "Well, we've got to do it for the old man."

In the late 1930s we had our problems, financial and otherwise. Phil called a meeting of the Steelworkers' staff, I believe in New York City, and proceeded to outline what the problems were and what our financial situation was. He commended them for their dedication and hard work. But he wound up by saying, "Now, I say to you, get off your fat rumps and go out there and do the job that has to be done!" So, after telling them how magnificent they were and how well they had done generally, he invited them to get off their rumps and go out and organize the unorganized. There was no resentment, just the feeling that the boss is right and we probably haven't given it the ultimate, and let's go out and do it!

Much reference has been made to the similarities and differences between Murray and Lewis. I did not know Lewis nearly as well as I knew Murray. I met Lewis on a number of occasions; I was impressed by him. He was a tremendous individual, a giant among giants, as was Phil Murray. But they were different in many respects. Lewis roared like a lion and shook the rafters. When he made his point, he made it very well. Phil Murray just talked. Sometimes you had to sit on the edge of your seat and hold your breath to hear what he was saying, but what he said was so important and so right and he said it so well that you did sit on the edge of your seat and hold your breath to hear him.

Nonetheless, both men were giants in the labor movement in their time. I don't think you can take that away from either one of them. I didn't know Lewis well enough to know how compassionate he was, but I think we came down a bit hard on John on that subject. I think he had a lot of compassion, and he was a dedicated labor leader. When someone went up to shake hands with him, more often than not he recognized him after the first or second time and always in parting would say, "Good seeing you, and my compliments to your membership." I think he meant it.

ABE RASKIN

Abe Raskin began his career as a labor reporter in the 1930s and for many years was with the New York Times *as a labor reporter, chief labor correspondent, and columnist, before concluding his career as assistant editorial page editor.*

Phil Murray was, beyond anybody I've known in the labor movement, and I've known practically everybody, a saintly figure. There was a quality in Phil, very well conveyed, as Walter Burke recalled, in that speech Murray delighted to make about the function of unionism in the home, to put carpets on the floor and provide a better break for the kids. This was very much in contrast to John L., who reveled in being captain of a thunderous host battling, and beating, the rich and powerful.

Before getting into the two points I really want to make, I wanted to say a little about the rift between Lewis and Phil Murray, which was extremely painful to Phil, no question. I don't know how painful it was to Lewis, probably not very, but it was a wrenching experience for Phil. Mel Dubofsky has said quite rightly that what tore their relationship apart was the surprise accouplement letter Lewis sent Murray shortly after Pearl Harbor. John L., who had torpedoed every overture toward AFL-CIO unity, had, up until the Japanese attack, lined up with the America Firsters to sabotage the defense effort, partly because of his rabid hatred for FDR. Suddenly, Lewis decided that patriotism required him to conjure up his defunct post as chairman of the CIO Peace Committee and propose a merger. He did not disclose that he had had some private meetings with fellow America Firster Big Bill Hutcheson of the AFL Carpenters' and Joiners' Union, whom he had once punched in the nose but who was now his great buddy. The letter was what tore them apart and, of course, led very shortly thereafter to Phil's angry reaction that he wasn't going to be "Pearl Harbored."

The whole point of the accouplement letter was to make George Meany president of the merged organization and to retire both Phil Murray and William Green, thus getting them off the scene. Phil reacted very harshly to that idea. But for two years prior to that, going back to 1940, when Lewis's rabid hostility toward

FDR was finding increasingly virulent expression, Phil tried, and succeeded in, keeping a low profile, while remaining committed to Roosevelt and admiring him. Phil left it to Sidney Hillman to mobilize the CIO forces in support of Roosevelt.

I remember Lewis sending Allan Haywood (a UMW/CIO aide to Lewis) up to Rochester to the state CIO convention in 1940. The left wing, of course, was very much on Lewis's side at that time. They defended the Nazi-Soviet pact, so Lewis's anti-Roosevelt position was very welcome to them. Allan was sent up to be the liaison between Lewis and Mike Quill, who was then the New York field marshall of the Moscow Firsters in the CIO.

The Hillman forces had a paper majority in the state CIO convention and had pushed through a resolution endorsing FDR. Mike Quill and the leftists then walked out of the convention and held a rump convention in the lobby of the hotel, while keeping in close touch with Allan, who was in the hotel room above. Quill denounced the pro-Roosevelt delegates as "paid gangsters" and said that their resolution could be written in toilet paper, for all the worth it had.

Phil, as I say, kept a very low profile through all of this period. Lewis, though, just before the election, endorsed Willkie and made a commitment to resign as CIO president if Willkie did not get in. The leftists tried hard at the Atlantic City convention, right after the election, to persuade Lewis to stay on. He made his infamous speech denouncing the Hillmans, the Dubinskys, the Zaritskys—very antisemitic talk—but being a proud man, he stuck with his decision to step down. Phil was chosen to succeed Lewis.

Phil then found himself more and more in tension with Lewis and the leftists, who, for differing reasons, were all sabotaging the defense effort. War was getting closer and closer. Many of the left wing's actions were very disruptive, and, of course, Lewis was forcing the issue. His strike in the captive coal mines, for instance, was threatening the whole position of the National Defense Mediation Board. Phil was very much on the spot; he was still a vice president of the United Mine Workers, and although he was not much in sympathy with the strike, he was officially, for the record, one hundred percent behind Lewis. Nonetheless, Lewis recognized that Murray was getting closer and closer to Hillman in support of the defense effort and the fight against the Axis powers. Then, in June 1941, came the rupture as a result of the signing of the Hitler-Stalin Pact, at which point the left wing switched one thousand percent and were as hostile as Hillman to the sabotage. In fact, they were for opening up a second front, for getting the United States into the war, and so on.

At the 1941 convention of the CIO in Detroit, Phil presided for the first time in his own right as president. Goons of Denny Lewis (John Lewis's brother) from District 50 were roaming the corridors of the Statler Hotel, beating up Phil Murray's people to the point where the UAW had to call out the Briggs Flying Squad to do battle with the thugs. It was a very, very painful period for Phil. When the accouplement letter came, it was very embarrassing for Phil to have to oppose a step put forward in the name of labor unity to advance the defense effort and painful for FDR, who had regularly called for unity at every convention and had just two weeks before Pearl Harbor, in November 1941, sent a letter to the convention of both the AFL and CIO saying: "Please unite the labor movement. There is every good reason from the standpoint of the workers of America to do it, but over and beyond that, the nation needs a unified labor movement in this time of military danger."

Suddenly, John L. comes along, the great scourge of unity, and proposes a merger and lines up the AFL in support of his move, because Hutcheson had enough clout to pull Bill Green and the rest of them along, even though Green was going to be one of the sacrifices. FDR had to come to Phil's rescue by executing a flanking maneuver. They created a united labor victory committee as an alternative to outright unity and got both the AFL and the CIO to agree to maintain a no-strike pledge through the duration of the war. That got everybody off the hook, and very shortly thereafter, as Mel Dubofksy recalled, Lewis summoned Phil to the United Mine Workers and the executive board kicked him out as vice president. It was a dreadful, dreadful period for Phil, but he didn't allow it to poison his life.

There are two more points I want to make. I'm not very happy with the discussion of the 1946 strike at this conference or with other discussions of that particular situation. True, every one of the great industrywide strikes in steel—1946, 1949, 1952, 1959, and so on—has been marked by total solidarity, and in that respect the Steelworkers have always been an inspiring force. But the strike in 1946, just after V-J Day, was a test for both labor and management.

I was in the Pentagon during the war, and I know all the thinking about the postwar period in the Pentagon, in the Navy Department, in the WPB, around Roosevelt, around Truman was on the problems of reconversion. The expectation was that there would be serious unemployment after the war and a tremendous loss of purchasing power. The trade union movement viewed itself as having two big challenges: one, to prove that it was not just a puppet of the War Labor Board that would collapse if it had to stand on its own, and, two, to maintain the purchasing power of its members. The big test was whether labor could meet the needs of its members without touching off a wave of inflation. The 1946 strike was basically not so much over wages in the end as whether there would be a price increase in steel. This issue had been posed by Walter Reuther in the General Motors strike, which started two months earlier. Phil resented Walter's calling the strike, and the Steelworkers' union in the end became the instrument for starting the wage-price spiral. In terms of labor's public position, that outcome was one of the things—almost as much as Lewis's wartime strikes and many of Lewis's actions right after the war—which gave labor a black eye. Coupled with the railroad strike and other upsets on the labor front, these developments led to Taft-Hartley and had a very unfortunate effect. So, while I admired Phil for his belief that he had to call the strike—the steel industry certainly gave him no option in that regard—his failure to stand up for the anti-inflation position that Reuther was fighting for was, I think, a classic failure of the trade union movement, for which it is still paying a price.

Now let me turn to my last point, which has to do with the quality of work life programs and labor-management participation teams. Lynn Williams has spoken with great hope of the new arrangements, particularly guaranteed employment and profit-sharing at National Steel, board representation at Wheeling-Pittsburgh, giving unions a voice in investment policies and strategic planning, providing complete information on a company's financial status, and so on. All of these programs, I think, are the way to go. I'm a thousand percent for them, and I admire the initiatives that the Steelworkers, the Auto Workers, and others are taking in that direction and the degree to which, in some companies at least, there is receptivity to them.

But while I applaud such moves toward greater participatory democracy in the workplace, it is delusive not to be well aware of the dark clouds that hang over the best of these plans. Never mind their collapse at Eastern Airlines. There is General Motors, where Irving Bluestone started putting the building blocks of a very good system in place more than a decade ago and where a lot of really good things have happened. Still, what real union power is there when the company can announce that it is going to shut down eleven plants. True, they gave the union notice and it will be a year and a half before the plants close, but twenty-nine thousand people will be affected, and it is very clear that that is only the beginning of a scaling down at General Motors. The degree to which the union has any real power to influence decisions of such magnitude seems to be about zero.

The Saturn plan, for example, was a marvelous concept. According to the advance buildup, the idea was that from day one the union would be a full partner and nothing would be done without the union having veto power. Now the Saturn plan is being cut back before they even build the plant, and I don't hear anybody in the union saying, "We were consulted about this. We are copartners in these decisions." So if you consider that and the mania for mergers that's going on—people are told one day, "You're full partners in this operation, everything revolves around you, you're the heartblood of this corporation," and the next day some remote multinational has acquired the company, takes a look at it, and says, "You don't fit in the combined balance sheet, get lost!"—what is the basis for the kind of trust that must underlie these very great plans?

JOHN HOERR

John Hoerr, a longtime senior labor writer for Business Week *magazine, covered the USWA while based in Pittsburgh for several years. Now an assistant editor, he is completing a book on the USWA in the 1980s.*

My remarks are built around the idea that SWOC started as a top-down organization. Professor Brody and Professor Dubofsky, and others too, have pointed this out. I think this organizational structure greatly influenced politics and collective bargaining policies and has caused problems that had to be addressed. I can think of one recent example. I started reporting on the steel industry in late 1964, just about the time that I. W. Abel, Walter Burke, and Joseph Molony began their campaign to unseat Dave McDonald. Although most people refer to that campaign as an executive board revolt and we heard a lot of rhetoric about McDonald and his country clubs, I was struck by another issue. I remember that Steelworker activists who supported the Abel-Burke-Molony ticket in the Monongahela Valley also talked of the need to resolve local issues. Under McDonald's industrywide bargaining setup, local unions had little opportunity to negotiate on working conditions in the plants. The top-down organization of the union left no room for local autonomy in bargaining. Abel said he would establish a local negotiating procedure.

When this issue was brought up at a press conference, McDonald said, "What local issues? They have a grievance procedure, don't they?" But the activists weren't talking about discharge cases and other complaints that could be settled in the grievance procedure. They wanted to improve conditions in the plants, safety and health conditions, for example. They wanted to negotiate changes in these conditions, not just file a complaint about them. They also wanted a voice in improving the production process and quality, issues that have become the nub of the quality of work life and participation movements. These guys didn't talk about such concepts, of course, and they certainly didn't talk about helping management cut costs. But they did talk about mismanagement in the plants and what could be done about it.

The activists I'm talking about were either World War II vets or had come out of school after the war and gone into the mills, the younger generation. They had, as each new generation does, different ideas about work and what they wanted out of it. They had been around more and had more education than the older generation of steelworkers, and they wanted more control over their lives and work in the mills. Today, we see the same attitude, though probably stronger, in the "baby-boom" generation.

In 1968, after Abel, Burke, and Molony were elected, they created a mechanism for bargaining on local issues. I think this is often forgotten. This team opened up the union to rank-and-file influence. It was a break from the top-down organizational style. It is true that there was no local right to strike. And it's certainly true that the companies held back on serious local issues until Abel negotiated an industrywide economic agreement. Then the companies said, "Well, now, you're not going to call an industrywide strike over parking lots at Homestead, are you?" In many cases, the unresolved local issues would get "washed out." I'm sure that Abel and Burke remember that. A lot of local union people complained about being "washed out." Some of them were demagogues, but others had legitimate complaints.

When Abel negotiated the Experimental Negotiating Agreement (ENA)—the no-strike agreement—in 1973, it contained the first local right-to-strike clause. That was a significant change and, I think, the feature that won ratification of the ENA by the Basic Steel Industry Conference.

What I'd like to do now is look at the top-down theme from another angle, starting in the 1930s. I'm currently working on a book about labor in the 1980s that focuses on the steel industry. I think the steel industry "lost it," and probably the union also, on the mill floor. The industry did not become competitive even as it finally began to realize in the 1960s and 1970s that foreign competition was growing. The companies didn't cut prices in the 1960s, when they might have. They were late in introducing the basic oxygen furnace and other technological improvements. But I think the real problem occurred on the mill floor.

The steel companies refused to work with the union. They had the "management is always right" attitude. I began hearing many younger steelworkers in the 1960s saying that "management won't listen to what we know we can do to produce steel better." Of course, the local people didn't send resolutions to the Wage Policy Committee saying, "We want a worker partic- ipation mechanism in the next contract." It's difficult to express in concrete terms a desire for participation when you've never had it. But the steel industry probably would be better off today if management and the union had worked together to make the plants more competitive. One issue I'm exploring in my book is why this did not happen.

The irony is that shortly after SWOC was formed in the 1930s, it promoted a remarkable effort to install worker participation. I'm not revealing something unknown. Sanford Jacoby has men- tioned the SWOC campaign in articles on union-management cooperation in the 1930s and 1940s. But I think it deserves more attention. I especially wanted to know why this program—it was a union policy, really—suddenly disappeared at the end of World War II. I did some research in various archives, including Penn State's, and I'd like to outline briefly what I have found.

Phil Murray appointed Clint Golden as the eastern regional director of SWOC in 1936. A self-educated man, Golden became interested in participation in the 1920s when he taught at Brook- wood Labor College. He also became enthusiastic about the B&O Plan, which consisted of labor-management committees that sug- gested work improvements. This was a legitimate, bona fide, independent union plan and did not deserve the label of com- pany union. Moreover, Golden, as a machinist, understood that workers could contribute a lot to improving the work process. Golden's associate in the SWOC program was Harold Rutten- berg, the research director of SWOC. A young intellectual, Rut- tenberg had helped the Amalgamated rank and filers try to take over that union in 1934. That experience, he told me, convinced him that rank-and-file workers "were full of all kinds of ideas as to how you could do things better and more economically."

One day in 1937, a SWOC lodge president named Joe Scanlon, who worked at Empire Steel Company in Mansfield, Ohio, showed up at Golden's office. With him were other workers and the president of Empire Steel. The company had just emerged from bankruptcy and could not pay a scheduled wage increase. What could be done? Golden suggested that the committee return to

Mansfield, interview each worker, and come up with ideas for cutting costs and making the plant more productive. Scanlon devised a way of eliciting information from the workers—no small undertaking in the 1930s when workers were highly suspicious of management. Within months, Empire was solvent and granted a wage increase.

On the basis of this experience, Golden brought Scanlon to Pittsburgh as head of a new industrial engineering department. In 1938, Golden, Scanlon, and Ruttenberg began a formal program of offering to help troubled companies through the participation process, although they seldom used this term. SWOC even produced a pamphlet called *Production Problems,* which was written by an assistant to Morris Cooke, a famous industrial engineer of the time. Four thousand copies of the pamphlet were printed and distributed to SWOC lodges, companies, academics, and government agencies. The pamphlet explained how union members could cooperate with management in improving the work process.

Professor Brody made a pertinent point to me in conversation. Ad hoc arrangements to cooperate were not rare, but unions often got no *quid pro quos* for participating on the shop floor. *Production Problems* sets forth four conditions for worker cooperation. First, management had to agree to the union shop, which was not all that common in the late 1930s. Second, no worker could lose his job as a result of improvements in practices or technology. Third, the union had to be involved with management at every step in the process. And fourth, the workers had to share in the gains resulting from the improvements, in short, a gain-sharing plan. These four points are also the cornerstones of the new participation agreements of the 1980s. SWOC advocated them nearly fifty years ago.

According to *Fortune,* which in 1950 published the best early summary of the SWOC program, Scanlon instituted cooperation programs at forty to fifty companies from 1938 to 1946. Most were small fabricating companies, and many had financial problems. The largest company was a basic steel producer with four thousand employees. It was from this experience that Scanlon got his idea of linking some measure of performance with participation. He eventually developed what became known as the

Scanlon Plan, of which there are several hundred in existence today.

Another step in the SWOC program came when Murray co-authored the book *Labor and Organized Production* with Morris Cooke. The book advocated cooperation and participation. But the nature of Murray's involvement indicates that he was by no means committed to union-management cooperation. Golden, who was a friend of Cooke's, apparently persuaded Murray to lend his name to the book. Murray wrote no part of it. About a dozen academics, consultants, SWOC staff members, and government technicians wrote various chapters, and Cooke put them together. In fact, Golden wrote many years later, Murray read very little of the book. Ruttenberg says that Murray was "intellectually honest" and could see that eventually labor would have to cooperate on the shop floor to keep productivity growing. In the short term, Murray saw that cooperation could help SWOC obtain a contract, the union shop, and dues-paying members.

The better book was Ruttenberg's and Golden's *The Dynamics of Industrial Democracy,* which came directly out of their experiences in the shops where they had set up participation committees. It provided a lot of nuts and bolts and had a strong brief for the union shop. The book also stated Golden's and Ruttenberg's philosophy, that if there were going to be wage increases, there had to be productivity growth.

During the war years, Murray pushed his industrial council proposal, which Ron Schatz outlined. This is another example of a top-down concept. It called for a "top scheduling clerk" who would coordinate all production throughout each basic industry. I think Schatz is absolutely correct in saying that Murray could not have thought that any company would possibly buy the idea. Of course, Donald Nelson of the War Production Board transformed the Murray Plan into his own proposal for establishing plant-level labor-management committees to help the war effort. Murray urged all Steelworker locals to participate. The record shows that not many of these committees had any meaningful participation because management didn't want workers poking into managerial areas. Management didn't want to give up any power, any authority.

It's not clear what happened to the SWOC participation program during the war. It was probably put aside, or subsumed by the labor-management committee approach. But it came to an end in 1946. The concept of worker participation disappeared for thirty-five years from the United Steelworkers, to be revived in 1980 with a contract provision calling for establishment of labor-management participation teams. What happened in the interim?

Golden and Ruttenberg both resigned in July of 1946 and Scanlon resigned a few months later. Golden, who by then was a vice president, left for a number of reasons. First, he didn't like the power politics that Lee Pressman and Dave McDonald were playing in the union. Second, he felt that Murray was a poor manager. It was difficult for Golden to carry out his administrative responsibilities in this politicized atmosphere. Third, and most important, according to Golden's biographer, Thomas Brooks, Golden couldn't carry out his cooperation program. "It seems," he wrote in his diary in May 1946, "that most of the effort Joe Scanlon and I particularly have put forth to advocate and to build cooperative relationships has been undone by our associates."

There is no evidence of an outright split between Murray and Golden. But they had very different views on the possibility of real labor-management cooperation. Murray did not trust business executives, whom he called "factotems" of the capitalists. Golden, according to USWA staff members who worked with him, leaned too far in the other direction. A tension existed between the two men on the subject. In November of 1946, Murray invited Golden to attend a Wage Policy Committee meeting. Murray made a strong speech condemning the idea that management wanted to get along peacefully with the union. In a letter to Scanlon, Golden said he felt the remarks were directed to him, especially when Murray concluded, "I do not want peace at any price!" Golden added: "As if anyone had suggested that he did."

Ruttenberg, by coincidence, resigned in the same week in July 1946. He claims to me that he left primarily because he didn't like the direction Murray intended to take the union in the postwar era. During the last years of the war, Ruttenberg says, he had many conversations with the USWA president about a long-term direction for collective bargaining. Ruttenberg believed that the union had to "assume joint responsibility with management for the economic health and success of the company." Murray, he claims, rejected this idea, saying that the time wasn't right and that management, in any case, was dead set against collaboration.

The two may have had those conversations. But union staffers who knew Ruttenberg tell a different story about his resignation. Ruttenberg was a very aggressive young man who, Golden felt, became arrogant as the assistant director of the steel division of the War Production Board. Moreover, Ruttenberg learned much in this position about the management and financial side of the steel industry. He told staffers that he wanted to make a lot of money. At the invitation of Cyrus Eaton, he left the union to become vice president of Portsmouth Steel Company.

With Golden and Ruttenberg gone, Scanlon had no support in the union for his ideas and the participation program. In October 1946, he accepted an invitation to join MIT's Industrial Relations Section. While teaching, Scanlon continued to help unions and companies install participation and gain-sharing plans. By the early 1950s, his plan was known as the Scanlon Plan.

As a journalist, I covered steel labor on a fairly intimate basis for ten years, starting in 1965. I never heard anybody in the United Steelworkers refer to Scanlon or to the early SWOC participation program. I never heard anybody say, "Why don't we bring it back?" I knew of Scanlon only through reading about him. It was as if the union wanted to forget the entire episode of union-management cooperation. The one exception was a tripartite committee and gain-sharing plan established at Kaiser Steel in the early 1960s. When the USWA attempted to explore the concept with other steel companies, it was rebuffed.

Of course, management in the early postwar years gave the Steelworkers every reason to shy away from cooperation. Coming out of the war, management embarked on a campaign to weaken the power of organized labor and went on to pass the Taft-Hartley Act in 1947. In the President's Labor-Management Conference of late 1945, the management side proposed that a long list of managerial functions be excluded from bargaining and the grievance procedure. Union representatives refused to accede to the demand.

It's hard to believe that Murray would have achieved very much had he pursued the idea of participation in the first half-decade or so after the war. And so, if you don't mind a speculative conclusion, I believe that the USWA took itself out of the workplace, leaving the grievance committeemen behind. It took itself away from the work process and left that to management. The union took the money and ran.

HAROLD J. RUTTENBERG

Harold J. Ruttenberg was an organizer and the research director of SWOC and the USWA from 1936 to 1946 and the assistant director of the steel division of the War Production Board for the years 1942–43.

I am not a historian. My comments and recollections are those of a person who was on the scene from September 1933 to July 1, 1946, as a participant in the USWA. I was an intimate of both Clinton S. Golden's and Philip Murray's, worked closely with Vincent Sweeney and Lee Pressman, was tolerated by Van A. Bittner, and came in occasional conflict with David J. McDonald. My departure from the USWA was over a fundamental policy and was followed a few weeks later by the resignations of Golden and Joseph Scanlon, whom we had brought into the Research Department from a steel mill. I am the last surviving member of this original leadership group. My duties as the union economist (my formal title) included being assistant to Clinton Golden until Philip Murray stole me away. The union put me in as a dollar-a-year assistant director of the steel division of the War Production Board, for 1942–43. The economic work of the Little Steel case fell to me, and I worked with Phil Murray and George Meany in challenging the cost-of-living index during the war.

Professor Melvyn Dubofsky calls Philip Murray and John L. Lewis "labor's odd couple" because they were so different yet complemented each other. In their years together in the miners' union, Murray was in charge of membership relations and Lewis was in charge of relations with management, financiers, politicians, and the media. When John L. gave Phil the job of unionizing the steelworkers, he retained for himself the functions of handling Washington and the "steel magnates," to use Phil's term for the men who ran the steel companies. They actually were not an odd couple. They were a typical number one and number two team that is found in most organizations.

There was no split between the two men. John L. just decided that he had had enough of being a labor leader and decided to become a banker. He had opposed FDR in 1940. Earlier, Lewis had suggested to FDR that they would make a great pair of candidates, and FDR had asked, "What position would you take, John?" Rejected by FDR, John L. supported Wendell Willkie, whose loss gave him the door to exit the CIO, use the UMW to buy a bank, and devote his remaining career to being one of the "men of finance." In the process, he gave the coal operators a green light to mechanize, leading to the consequent precipitous decline in the number of coal miners. Lewis helped organize the coal miners as a vehicle to power. He never was a real coal miner, though he had worked briefly in a mine. In contrast, Phil was devoted to the betterment of his fellow men.

Professor Dubofsky fails to mention Phil's exposure to the Fabian Society in Scotland before he came to America. This was the key to his strength and the cause of his historic failure. This man of his people, who had a touch of greatness, a Lincolnesque quality about him, was a working-class individual. He firmly believed in the class struggle. His brilliant pragmatism could not cross what he perceived as the "Great Divide." Deep down, he could not trust "the employer."

Phil Murray and Clint Golden were a couple of socialists who worked together in organizing the steelworkers. They had a deep regard for each other and were an effective team, but eventually they separated over contrasting views on the role of the steelworkers' union in American industry. Clint had become an intellectual who outgrew his doctrinaire socialism. Phil was a natural leader who could not overcome his socialist learning that the bosses cannot be trusted, that management is tricky, and that capitalists are exploiters of labor.

Their first disagreement over "the other side" was in 1937 at Mesta Machine in West Homestead, Pennsylvania, where the SWOC local had struck. Clint decided that the workers should go back to work. Murray argued that if SWOC did not get a contract before the strike ended, they would lose the opportunity to unionize Mesta for a generation. Clint trusted management's word. He sent the men back to work. Mesta was not unionized for another generation. For the decade that I worked with and between Phil and Clint, "Mesta" was a buzz word.

The Myron Taylor-John L. Lewis agreement of 1937 was a surprise to Phil, Golden, Sweeney, and myself only in timing. John L. kept it quiet, lest a failure expose him. But we all knew that U.S. Steel was SWOC's first objective. When the idea of capturing the company unions was spelled out to John L., he grabbed it with enthusiasm. I had mentioned it as early as 1934, when I was working on a Brookings study of the steel industry and I could see the appeal of the men in the Monongahela Valley who had risen to the top of the employee representation plans. When SWOC was created, the strategy of winning over these men was *the* priority in which I played a part. In the months preceding the Taylor agreement, Lewis kept asking how we were doing.

I remember reporting on progress at Jones & Laughlin and John L. asking impatiently for a progress report on Carnegie-Illinois. We knew that his first target was U.S. Steel. We knew that we had to take over the company unions. What we did not know was that a diplomatic move could sign up U.S. Steel. Lee Pressman, who naturally had some of Lewis's views of man, took great delight in phoning me to break the news. His testimony that it came as a complete surprise to Phil is not entirely correct, though it probably was to the best of Lee's knowledge. Tom Kennedy, secretary of the UMW, had told Phil that John L. was talking to Myron Taylor, but Phil dismissed it. His distrust of "the other side" told him that only a successful strike could force U.S. Steel to recognize the union. Phil was wrong on this as he was about "the other side."

Lee Pressman's testimony, cited by Professor Dubofsky, on the start of the 1937 Little Steel strike is a view from Washington. Lee's testimony that Phil did not clear with John L. on the strike runs counter to the fact that Tom Girdler, the chief executive officer of Republic Steel, provoked it and John L. knew all about that. Lee is correct that we took "a terrific drubbing." Phil had to go west for a rest while John Owens, head of the UMW in Ohio, was sent in by John L. to get the Bethlehem-Inland-Youngstown plants back to work. The big story for historians is that via democratic, legal means SWOC was able in a few years to sign up the Little Steel companies thanks, in large part, to the developing war economy and the "all shoulders to the wheel" patriotism that the war unleashed.

For a year before I left the union, in July 1946, I had been in deep discussion with Phil about the future. While he intellectually could comprehend the merits of my contentions, he could not bring himself to expose himself to the "goodwill of the Steel Magnates." Phil did not trust them. But Phil could write me, as he did in his July 2, 1946, farewell letter, that "I am hopeful that your new associations will provide opportunity for you to build up those fine constructive labor-management relations that ought to prevail in the American industry."

My contentions were quite simple and clear, namely, that the combined economic and political power of the USWA could result in cost increases for the "magnates" beyond their ability to pass them on in price increases or to offset them with capital improvements. Once the companies began to absorb these cost increases, their profits would decline, adversely affecting their borrowing power to make capital improvements. When the decline set in, the employment among the steelworkers would drop; even retirees could be hurt. It was therefore important that the USWA develop a program to tie employment costs to productivity. If, as we knew, the "magnates" would not agree, my analysis went, the USWA could force them to engage in union-management cooperation to raise productivity on a sharing-with-labor basis, because, if I was correct that the USWA could push them to the wall by "more-more" bargaining, then the combined economic and political power of the USWA could force them into productivity bargaining with sharing.

I got nowhere. Phil ended the discussion, saying that I probably was correct but that it wouldn't happen in his lifetime. I could stay on only by following union policy. Phil wanted no internecine squabbles. My leaving led to Clint and Joe Scanlon's departure shortly thereafter. Each, in his own way, pursued his dream but lacked the power to do very much about it.

The papers fail to mention, some even to comprehend, that this basic dispute was at the heart of the internal postwar discussion inside the Steelworkers' union. Before the basic steel industry debacle, this issue was very sensitive, certainly for labor leaders and even historians. But now that the steel house of cards has collapsed, labor historians, I would hope, can and will tackle this phase of the history of the USWA and how the outcome could have been different.

Phil Murray was a soft-spoken man with a genuine compassion

for his fellow man, but he was also tough as nails. Many men testified that if they had to be fired, they would rather have had Phil do it than John L. But the implication that Phil was less tough than John L. is not borne out by my recollections. As an example, some time late in 1936, I had returned from Weirton. Paul Rusen, the district director, had been roughed up. I remember visiting him at his home. One of the organizers with us asked me to intercede with Phil to get Rusen transferred to another district. I did. Phil said, "I'll transfer him, all right, right out of the organization. Harold, you never know whether a man is made out of steel or sh-- until he is in a crisis. Most of us function well in our routine work. It is in a crisis that our mettle is tested."

I take exception to tying Phil's death in 1952 to Adlai Stevenson's not being elected. Phil could have led his troops under President Eisenhower with the greatest of ease. His 1941 infarction was serious. It was before the heart-lung machine was in use for bypass cardiac surgery. Phil lived eleven years with serious heart muscle damage, which compares favorably with the postinfarction survival rate before the heart-lung machine.

BIBLIOGRAPHY

Abel, I. W. *Collective Bargaining: Labor Relations in Steel, Then and Now*. New York: Columbia University Press, 1976.

Augustine, Thomas. "The Negro Steelworkers of Pittsburgh and the Unions." Ph.D. diss., University of Pittsburgh, 1948.

Bernstein, Irving. *The Turbulent Years: A History of American Workers, 1933–1941*. Boston: Houghton-Mifflin, 1969.

Bodnar, John. *Immigration and Industrialization: Ethnicity in an American Mill Town, 1870–1940*. Pittsburgh: University of Pittsburgh Press, 1977.

_____. "Immigration, Kinship, and the Rise of Working-Class Realism in Industrial America." *Journal of Social History* 14 (Fall 1980):45–59.

_____. *Lives of Their Own: Blacks, Italians and Poles in Pittsburgh, 1900–1960*. Pittsburgh: University of Pittsburgh Press, 1982.

"Brief Biography of Francis Feehan." *See* John Brophy Papers.

Brody, David. "The CIO after 50 Years: A Historical Reckoning." *Dissent* (Fall 1985):457–72.

_____. *Labor in Crisis*. Philadelphia: Lippincott, 1965.

_____. *Workers in Industrial America: Essays on the Twentieth Century Struggle*. New York: Oxford University Press, 1980.

Brooks, Robert R. *As Steel Goes: Unionism in a Basic Industry*. New Haven: Yale University Press, 1940.

_____. *Clint: A Biography of a Labor Intellectual*. New York: Atheneum, 1978.

Brooks, Thomas R. *Toil and Trouble: A History of American Labor*. 2d ed. New York: Delacorte Press, 1971.

Brophy, John. *A Miner's Life*. Madison: University of Wisconsin Press, 1964.

_____. Papers. Catholic University of America, Washington, D.C.

Cayton, Horace R., and George S. Mitchell. *The Black Workers and the New Unions*. Chapel Hill: University of North Carolina Press, 1939.

Chamberlain, Neil W. *The Union Challenge to Management Control*. New York: Harper, 1948.

Childs, Marquis. Interview, 1958. Oral History Collection, Columbia University, New York.

Coleman, Glenn McKinley. "The Growth of Management-Labor Understanding in the Steel Industry of Western Pennsylvania with Special Emphasis on Jobs Security and Seniority." Ph.D. diss., University of Pittsburgh, 1952.

Conner, Valerie Jean. *The National War Labor Board: Stability, Social Justice, and the Voluntary State in World War I*. Chapel Hill: University of North Carolina Press, 1983.

Cooke, Morris Llewellyn, and Philip Murray. *Organized Labor and Production: Next Steps in Industrial Democracy*. New York: Harper and Brothers, 1940.

Dawley, Alan. *Class and Community: The Industrial Revolution in Lynn*. Cambridge: Harvard University Press, 1976.

DeCaux, Len. *Labor Radical: From the Wobblies to the CIO*. Boston: Beacon Press, 1970.

Dickerson, Dennis Clark. "Black Steelworkers in Western Pennsylvania, 1915–1950." Ph.D. diss., Washington University, 1978.

_____. *Out of the Crucible: Black Steelworkers in Western Pennsylvania, 1875–1980*. Albany: State University of New York Press, 1986.

Draham, Anne-Marie, Jim Dougherty, and Irwin Marcus. "People, Power and Profits: The Struggle of U.S. Steel Workers for Economic Democracy, 1892–1985." Unpublished manuscript.

Dubofsky, Melvyn, and Warren Van Tine. *John L. Lewis: A Biography*. New York: Quadrangle/New York Times Books, 1977.

Durand, John P. *The Labor Force in the United States, 1890–1940*. New York: Social Science Research Council, 1948.

Edwards, P. K. *Strikes in the United States, 1881–1974*. New York: St. Martin's Press, 1981.

Ellickson, Katherine Pollack. Papers. Franklin D. Roosevelt Library, Hyde Park, New York.

Erickson, Ethel. *Women's Employment in the Making of Steel, 1943.* Bulletin Numbers 192–195. Washington, D.C.: Women's Bureau, Department of Labor, 1944.

Fink, Gary. *Biographical Dictionary of American Labor Leaders.* Westport, Conn.: Greenwood Press, 1974.

Fink, Leon. "The Uses of Political Power: Toward a Theory of the Labor Movement in the Era of the Knights of Labor." In *Working-Class America: Essays on Labor, Community, and American Society,* edited by Michael Frisch and Daniel J. Walkowitz. Urbana: University of Illinois Press, 1983.

Foster, James Caldwell. *The Union Politic: The CIO Political Action Committee.* Columbia: University of Missouri Press, 1975.

Foster, William Z. *Organizing Steel.* New York: International Publishers, 1936.

Fraser, Steve. "Dress Rehearsal for the New Deal: Shop-Floor Insurgents, Political Elites, and Industrial Democracy in the Amalgamated Clothing Workers." In *Working-Class America: Essays on Labor, Community, and American Society,* edited by Michael Frisch and Daniel J. Walkowitz. Urbana: University of Illinois Press, 1983.

Friedlander, Peter. *The Emergence of a UAW Local, 1936–1939.* Pittsburgh: University of Pittsburgh Press, 1975.

Galenson, Walter. *The CIO Challenge to the AFL: A History of the American Labor Movement, 1935–1941.* Cambridge: Harvard University Press, 1960.

Germer, Adolph. Papers. State Historical Society of Wisconsin, Madison.

Gerstle, Gary. "The Mobilization of the Working Class Community: The Independent Textile Union in Woonsocket, 1931–1946." *Radical History Review* 17 (Spring 1978):161–67.

Goldberg, Arthur J. *AFL-CIO: Labor United.* New York: McGraw-Hill, 1956.

Golden, Clinton S., and Harold J. Ruttenberg. *The Dynamics of Industrial Democracy.* New York: Harper and Brothers, 1942.

Gottlieb, Peter. *Making Their Own Way: Southern Blacks Migration to Pittsburgh, 1916–1930.* Urbana: University of Illinois Press, 1987.

Grogan, William. *John Riffe*. New York: Coward-McCann, 1959.

Harbison, Frederick. "Labor Relations in the Iron and Steel Industry, 1937 to 1939." Ph.D. diss., Princeton University, 1940.

———. "Steel." In *How Collective Bargaining Works*, edited by Harry A. Millis. New York: Twentieth Century Fund, 1942.

Hawley, Ellis W. *The New Deal and the Problem of Monopoly: A Study in Economic Ambivalence*. Princeton, N.J.: Princeton University Press, 1966.

Herling, John. *Right to Challenge: People and Power in the Steelworkers Union*. New York: Harper and Row, 1972.

Hogan, William T. *Economic History of the Iron and Steel Industry in the United States*. 3 vols. Lexington, Mass.: Lexington Books, 1971.

"It Happened in Steel." *Fortune* 14 (May 1937):91–94.

Keck, Frank. "The Development of Labor Representation at the Homestead Steel Works." M.A. thesis, University of Pittsburgh, 1950.

Kelley, George. *Man of Steel: The Story of David J. McDonald*. New York: North American Book, 1954.

Kempton, Murray. "Ninth Annual Joseph P. Molony Memorial Lecture." University of Notre Dame, October 8, 1986.

Korson, George. *Coal Dust on the Fiddle*. Hatboro, Penn.: Folklore Associates, 1965.

Lauck, Jeff. Papers. University of Virginia, Charlottesville.

Levenstein, Harvey. *Communism, Anticommunism, and the CIO*. Westport, Conn.: Greenwood Press, 1981.

Lichtenstein, Nelson. "Auto Worker Militancy and the Structure of Factory Life, 1937–1955. *Journal of American History* 67 (September 1980):335–53.

———. *Labor's War at Home: The CIO in World War Two*. New York: Cambridge University Press, 1982.

Livernash, Robert E. *Collective Bargaining in the Basic Steel Industry: A Study of the Public Interest and the Role of the Government*. Washington, D.C.: U.S. Department of Labor, 1961.

Lubell, Samuel. *The Future of American Politics*. 3d ed. New York: Harper and Row, 1965.

Lynd, Alice, and Staughton Lynd. *Rank and File: Personal Histories of Working Class Organizers*. Boston: Beacon Press, 1973.

Lynd, Staughton. "The Possibility of Radicalism in the Early

1930s: The Case of Steel." In *Workers' Struggles Past and Present, A "Radical America" Reader,* edited by James Green. Philadelphia: Temple University Press, 1983.

Marcus, Maeva. *Truman and the Steel Seizure Case: The Limits of Presidential Power.* New York: Columbia University Press, 1977.

McDonald, David J. *Union Man.* New York: E. P. Dutton, 1969.

McQuaid, Kim. *Big Business and Presidential Power: From FDR to Reagan.* New York: Morrow, 1982.

Mills, C. Wright. *The New Men of Power: America's Labor Leaders.* New York: Harcourt Brace, 1948.

Montgomery, David. *Workers' Control in America: Studies in the History of Work, Technology, and Labor Struggles.* Cambridge: Harvard University Press, 1979.

Murray, Philip. "The Case of the West Virginia Coal Mine Workers." Opening statement before the Committee on Education and Labor of the U.S. Senate, October 1921. UMWA, 1921.

_____. *Organized Labor and Production.* New York: Harper and Brothers, 1940.

Nelson, Bruce. " 'Pentecost' on the Pacific: Maritime Workers and Working-Class Consciousness in the 1930s." *Political Power and Social Theory* 4 (1984):141–82.

Nelson, Daniel. "Origins of the Sit-Down Era: Worker Militancy and Innovation in the Rubber Industry, 1934–1938." *Labor History* 23 (Spring 1982):198–225.

Nyden, Philip. *Steelworkers Rank-and-File: The Political Economy of a Union Reform Movement.* New York: Praeger, 1984.

Peterson, Florence. *Strikes in the United States.* Washington, D.C.: U.S. Government Printing Office, 1937.

Pollak, Katherine. "Summary of Situation in Steel." Unpublished manuscript, Pennsylvania State University, 1936.

Preis, Art. *Labor's Giant Step: Twenty Years of the CIO.* New York: Pioneer Publishers, 1964.

Pressman, Lee. Interview, 1958. Oral History Collection, Columbia University, New York.

Randall, Clarence B. *A Creed for Free Enterprise.* Boston: Houghton-Mifflin, 1952.

Rawick, George. "Working-Class Self Activity." In *Workers' Struggles Past and Present, A "Radical America" Reader,* edited by James Green. Philadelphia: Temple University Press, 1983.

Rowan, Richard. *The Negro in the Steel Industry.* Philadelphia: University of Pennsylvania Press, 1968.

Ruck, Robert. "Origins of the Seniority System in Steel." Unpublished manuscript, 1975.

Ruttenberg, Harold J. Papers. Pennsylvania State University, University Park.

Sabadasz, Joel. "Parameters of Workers' Consciousness: Municipal Elections of 1937–41 in McKeesport, Clairton and Duquesne." Unpublished manuscript, 1986.

Schatz, Ronald W. "American Labor and the Catholic Church, 1919–1950." *International Labor and Working-Class History* 20 (Fall 1981):46–53.

――――. *The Electrical Workers: A History of Labor at General Electric and Westinghouse, 1920–1960.* Urbana: University of Illinois Press, 1983.

――――. "Philip Murray and the Subordination of the Industrial Unions to the United States Government." In *Labor Leaders in America,* edited by Melvyn Dubofsky and Warren Van Tine. Urbana: University of Illinois Press, 1987.

Schratz, Walter Alfred. "Development of and Experience with Industrial Grievance Procedure, with Reference to the Open-End and Closed-End Types." Ph.D. diss., University of Pittsburgh, 1954.

Spencer, Robert C. "Bargaining with the Government: A Case Study in the Politics of Collective Bargaining in the Basic Steel Industry." Ph.D. diss., University of Chicago, 1955.

The Steel Case: Industry Statements Presented to the Steel Panel of the National War Labor Board. n.p., 1944.

"The Steelworkers." *Fortune* (February 1944):164–66.

Stieber, Jack W. *The Steel Industry Wage Structure: A Study of the Joint Union-Management Job Evaluation Program in the Basic Steel Industry.* Cambridge: Harvard University Press, 1959.

Stone, Katherine. "The Origins of Job Structures in the Steel Industry." *Radical America* (November–December 1973):19–64.

Sweeney, Vincent D. *The United Steelworkers of America.* Pittsburgh: USWA, 1956.

Taft, Philip. *The A.F. of L. in the Time of Gompers.* New York: Harper, 1957.

_____. *The Structure and Government of Labor Unions.* Cambridge: Harvard University Press, 1956.

Tate, Juanita Diffay. "Philip Murray as a Labor Leader." Ph.D. diss., New York University, 1962.

Tilove, Robert. *Collective Bargaining in the Steel Industry.* Philadelphia: University of Pennsylvania Press, 1948.

Tomlins, Christopher L. *The State and the Unions: Labor Relations, Law, and the Organized Labor Movement in America, 1880–1960.* Cambridge: Harvard University Press, 1985.

Ulman, Lloyd. *The Government of the Steelworkers' Union.* New York: John Wiley, 1962.

_____. "Influence of the Economic Environment on the Structure of the Steel Workers' Union." In *Proceedings of the Industrial Relations Research Association* 14 (1961):227–37.

U.S. Department of Labor. *Collective Bargaining in the Basic Steel Industry: A Study of the Public Interest and the Role of Government.* Washington, D.C.: U.S. Department of Labor, 1961.

United Steelworkers. *In the Matter of Steel Workers Organizing Committee and Bethlehem Steel Company, Case 30, Republic Steel Corporation, Case 31 . . . (and others).* Submitted by Steel Workers Organizing Committee. Indianapolis: Cornelius Printing, 1943(?).

_____. *In re: United Steelworkers of America and United Steel Corporation, et al.* Brief submitted by the United Steelworkers of America to panel of National War Labor Board. Washington, 1944.

Walker, Charles. *Steeltown: An Industrial Case History of the Conflict between Progress and Security.* New York: Harper and Brothers, 1950.

Whyte, William F. *Pattern for Industrial Peace.* New York: Harper and Brothers, 1951.

MAJOR EVENTS IN THE HISTORY OF THE STEELWORKERS, 1933–85

June 16, 1933	President Franklin D. Roosevelt signs National Industrial Recovery Act, which includes employees' right to form unions
June 16–30, 1933	Steel companies establish employee representation plans
June–October 1933	Steelworkers flock to join Amalgamated Association of Iron, Steel, and Tin Workers (AA)
April 17, 1934	AA rank and file demand recognition of union by steel companies and threaten to strike if demand is refused
May–June 1934	AA rank-and-file movement loses momentum; strike call is canceled
January 3, 1935	Delegates from fifty rebellious AA lodges reconstitute rank-and-file steelworkers' movement
July 5, 1935	National Labor Relations Act (Wagner Act) passed, giving workers the right to bargain collectively
September 1935	Development of area joint councils of employee representatives in Pittsburgh-Youngstown and Calumet regions

November 1935	Formation of the Committee for Industrial Organization (CIO)
January–April 1936	Formation of Pittsburgh-Youngstown councils of U.S. Steel employee representation plans
May 1936	Collapse of plans to establish joint American Federation of Labor–AA organizing drive among steelworkers
June 4, 1936	Agreement reached between AA and CIO to organize steelworkers
June 17, 1936	Steel Workers' Organizing Committee (SWOC)—CIO formed in Pittsburgh, with Philip Murray as head
August 1, 1936	Publication of the first issue of SWOC's official newspaper, *Steel Labor*
August 25, 1936	Committee of employee representatives in U.S. Steel Pittsburgh-Youngstown area mills votes to demand wage increase
August 26, 1936	First SWOC charter in Canada issued to Local 1005 in Hamilton, Ontario
November 9, 1936	SWOC captures leadership of joint conferences of management and employee representatives in U.S. Steel
January 17, 1937	First meeting of Wage Policy Committee of SWOC
March 26, 1937	SWOC signs first contract with a major steel producer (Carnegie-Illinois)
April 12, 1937	U.S. Supreme Court upholds 1935 Wagner Act in case involving discharged SWOC members in Aliquippa, Pennsylvania
May 12–20, 1937	Jones & Laughlin Steel employees win strike and vote for SWOC in National Labor Relations Board election
May 26, 1937	SWOC strikes against Little Steel companies
May 30, 1937	Memorial Day massacre at Republic Steel in Chicago

October 1940	Bethlehem Steel organizing drive begins
November 1940	Philip Murray, chairman of SWOC, is elected president of the CIO, following John L. Lewis's resignation
December 13, 1940	First white-collar local organized in SWOC by office employees at U.S. Steel's National Tube Company
February 1941	SWOC Canadian organizing drive accelerates, following contract settlement at National Steel Car Company
March 29, 1941	Youngstown Sheet & Tube Company reinstates strikers fired in 1937, with back wages
May 15, 1941	SWOC wins National Labor Relations Board election at Bethlehem Steel's Lackawanna mill
May 19, 1942	SWOC convention in Cleveland adopts constitution and becomes United Steelworkers of America; Philip Murray elected president
July 16, 1942	U.S. War Labor Board issues formula for wage increases in wartime, based on decision in USWA–Little Steel dispute
August 1942	Inland Steel, Youngstown Sheet & Tube, Bethlehem Steel, and Republic Steel sign contracts with USWA
January 12, 1943	Beginning of first industrywide Canadian steel strike
April 1944	USWA officially recognized as collective bargaining agent at Steel Company of Canada
June 4, 1944	Aluminum Workers of America merges with USWA
February 13, 1945	First referendum election held for USWA International and district officers
January 21, 1946	Nationwide steel strike of 750,000 workers begins

October 1946	Wage inequity agreement reached between USWA and U.S. Steel
April 22, 1947	"Era of Good Feeling" contract signed between USWA and U.S. Steel
October 31, 1949	USWA and Bethlehem Steel reach first agreement in steel industry for company-financed pension plan
April 8, 1952	President Harry Truman declares government takeover of steel mills in union-industry wage dispute
November 9, 1952	Death of Philip Murray
March 11, 1953	David J. McDonald installed as new president of the USWA
June 12, 1953	USWA–U.S. Steel agreement wipes out differential wage rates between North and South
November 17, 1953	Beginning of McDonald-Fairless (president of U.S. Steel) joint tour of steel mills to promote better labor relations
August 1955	USWA wins supplementary unemployment benefits for first time in can industry contract
February 7, 1957	David McDonald defeats Donald Rarick for president of the USWA in referendum election
July 15, 1959	540,000 steelworkers begin strike, which will last for 116 days, against eleven major steel companies
October 1959	Kaiser Steel signs contract with USWA, leading to settlements between union and other steel companies in 1959 strike
January 1960	Formation of joint USWA–steel industry Human Relations Research Committee
April 10–17, 1962	"Steel Crisis": President John F. Kennedy demands rollback of steel price increases following signing of union contract

January 1963	Inauguration of USWA–Kaiser Steel productivity and profit-sharing plan
November 1964	I. W. Abel, Walter Burke, and Joseph Molony declare candidacies for USWA International offices
February 9, 1965	Election held between I. W. Abel and David McDonald; Abel elected president
September 1966	Industry conferences initiated by USWA as new vehicle for establishing collective bargaining policy
January 1967	International Union of Mine, Mill and Smelter Workers merges with USWA
February 23, 1968	End of seven-month strike in North American nonferrous industry
January 2, 1970	USWA merges with United Stone and Allied Products Workers
April 23, 1971	USWA merges with District 50, Allied and Technical Workers of America
March 28–29, 1973	Experimental Negotiating Agreement (ENA) ratified by USWA and major steel companies
April 12, 1974	Consent decree reached between nine steel companies and USWA to provide equal employment for minority workers
February 11, 1977	Lloyd McBride defeats Edward Sadlowski in referendum election for president
November 6, 1983	McBride dies; Lynn Williams named acting president
March 29, 1984	Williams defeats Frank McKee in referendum election
October 21, 1985	USWA merges with Upholsterers International Union

CONTRIBUTORS

David Brody is a professor of history at the University of California, Davis, a position he has held since 1967. A frequent contributor to books and journals, he is also the coeditor of the Working Class in American History Series, published by the University of Illinois Press. Among the books he has authored are *Steelworkers in America: The Non-Union Era* and *Workers in Industrial America: Essays on the Twentieth Century Struggle.*

Melvyn Dubofsky is a professor of history and sociology and chair of the history department at the State University of New York, Binghamton. He is the author of numerous books and essays in American labor and social history, including *A History of the IWW, John L. Lewis: A Biography,* and *When Workers Organize,* and the editor of *Labor Leaders in Industrial America* and *American Labor since the New Deal.* He has taught at the University of Massachusetts; the University of Wisconsin, Milwaukee; Northern Illinois University; Tel Aviv University; and the University of Warwick, England.

Ronald L. Filippelli is a professor and chair of the Department of Labor Studies and Industrial Relations at Pennsylvania State University. He received his Ph.D. in American history from Pennsylvania State University in 1970. From 1967 to 1982, he was the university's labor archivist in charge of the Pennsylvania Historical Collections and Labor Archives. He is the author of *Labor in the USA: A History* and of numerous professional and scholarly articles.

Mark McColloch is the labor archivist and an associate professor of history at the University of Pittsburgh, where he received his Ph.D. in 1975. He has worked as a welfare caseworker and taught at the Community College of Allegheny County. He is the author of *White Collar Labor in Transition* and of the chapter on the mid-twentieth century in the *History of Labor in Pennsylvania*.

Ronald W. Schatz is an associate professor of history at Wesleyan University, where he has taught since 1979. His research interests include the emergence of unions at the shop-floor level in the 1930s, communism and Catholicism among unionists, corporatist motifs in business and labor thought, and the development of the field of industrial relations. He is the author of *The Electrical Workers: A History of Labor at General Electric and Westinghouse, 1920–1960*.

EDITORS

Paul F. Clark is assistant professor and labor education coordinator in the Department of Labor Studies and Industrial Relations at Pennsylvania State University. He received his master's degree from the New York State School of Industrial and Labor Relations, Cornell University, and his Ph.D. from the University of Pittsburgh. He has also done graduate work at the University of Glasgow, Scotland. He is the author of *The Miners' Fight for Democracy: Arnold Miller and the Reform of the United Mine Workers.*

Peter Gottlieb is head of the Historical Collections and Labor Archives, Pattee Library, Pennsylvania State University, where he is responsible for the United Steelworkers of America Archives. Before joining Pennsylvania State University, Gottlieb served as associate curator of the West Virginia Collection at West Virginia University Library. He received his master's and Ph.D. degrees from the University of Pittsburgh and is the author of *Making Their Own Way: Southern Blacks' Migration to Pittsburgh, 1916–1930.*

Donald Kennedy is a program developer and trainer with the International Association of Machinists, Placid Harbor Education Center, Hollywood, Maryland. He has also been an assistant professor and the labor education coordinator in the Department of Labor Studies and Industrial Relations at Pennsylvania State University. He received his master's degree from Pennsylvania State University and did additional graduate work at the University of Michigan. He has edited several publications, including *Labor and Technology, Labor and Reindustrialization,* and the *Guide to Employment Legislation in Pennsylvania.*

145

INDEX

Library of Congress Cataloging in Publication Data

Forging a union of steel.

  Based on papers presented at a symposium held on
Nov. 13–14, 1986 and sponsored by the Dept. of Labor Studies at
Penn State University and others.
  Bibliography: p.
  Includes index.
  1. United Steelworkers of America—History—
Congresses.   2. Steel Workers Organizing Committee
(U.S.)—History—Congresses.   3. Murray, Philip,
1886–1952—Congresses.   4. Trade-unions—Iron and
steel workers—United States—History—Congresses.
I. Clark, Paul F., 1954– .   II. Gottlieb, Peter, 1949– .
III. Kennedy, Donald.   IV. Pennsylvania State
University. Dept. of Labor Studies.
HD6515.I5F58   1987   331.88'169142'0973   87-21508
ISBN 0-87546-134-4
ISBN 0-87546-135-2 (pbk.)